CogAT Test Prep Series

NON-VERBAL BATTERY

FIGURE ANALOGIES

Grade 2

A step by step STUDY GUIDE

by

MindMine

Why this book?

Cognitive abilities test **isn't an IQ test.** Cognitive abilities are brain-based skills related with the mechanisms of learning, memorizing, and paying attention rather than actual knowledge that was learned. **The more you practice, the more you develop** your cognitive flexibility.

- This book is designed to teach concepts and skills in a way kids understand with ease.

- Concepts are taught step by step and introduced incrementally.

- The focus of this book is to provide a solid foundation to fundamental skills. All the skills taught in the book will collectively increase the knowledge and will help kids to prepare and take the test confidently.

- Practice tests that are available in the market may not provide all the concepts needed. This book is aimed to give both concepts and practice.

Who should buy this book?

- 2nd graders taking CogAT (Form-7 Level-8)

- 1st graders planning to take CogAT (Any Form)

- 1st, 2nd and 3rd graders seeking to enrich their ANALYTICAL skills

📚 What is covered?

This book extensively covers **FIGURE ANALOGIES** section of **Non-Verbal Battery** (Approximately 220 unique questions) and another 250 secondary questions.

📖 2 FULL LENGTH PRACTICE TESTS with Answers

Full Length Practice Test#1   20 Questions

Full Length Practice Test#2   20 Questions

📖 FIGURE ANALOGIES

Change NUMBER of SIDES	25 Questions
Change COLOR	15 Questions
Change SIZE	25 Questions
FLIP (Reflection)	20 Questions
CUT	10 Questions
ADD / REMOVE	20 Questions
MOVE	15 Questions
SWAP	20 Questions
TURN	30 Questions

📚 Table of Contents

ANSWERS   Page#

FIGURE ANALOGIES

Find the figure that should go in the box with Question Mark

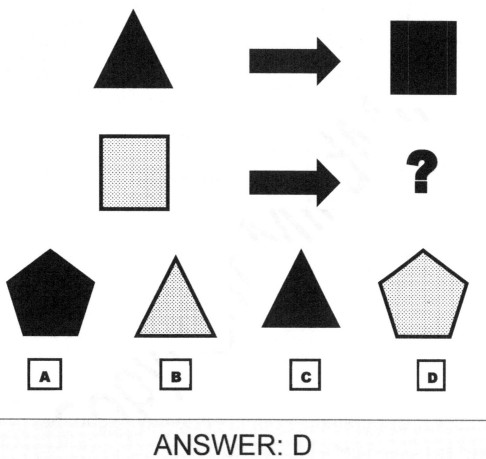

ANSWER: D

FIGURE ANALOGIES

HOW TO SOLVE?

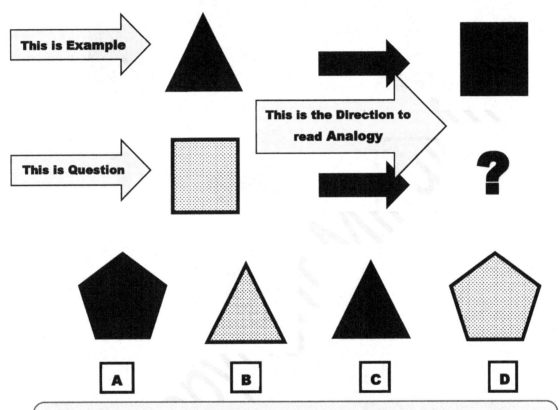

This is Example

This is Question

This is the Direction to read Analogy

?

A   B   C   D

STEP#1: Understand example Analogy. Read the way arrow is pointed (LEFT to RIGHT)

STEP#2: Apply same Analogy to question. Read the way arrow is pointed (LEFT to RIGHT).

**DO NOT Copy Example characteristics (such as Shape, Color, Pattern, Size, Position, Sides, Angle etc.,)

FIGURE ANALOGIES

HOW TO SOLVE?

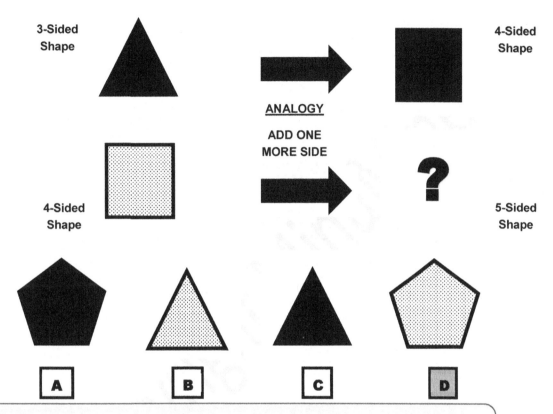

3-Sided Shape

4-Sided Shape

ANALOGY

ADD ONE MORE SIDE

4-Sided Shape

5-Sided Shape

?

A   B   C   D

STEP#1: Analogy: **Add one more side** (3-sided shape becomes a 4-sided shape)

STEP#2: Apply Analogy: **4-sided shape becomes a 5-sided shape**, when one more side is added. **Answer Choices B & C are WRONG**

DO NOT Copy Example characteristics (such as Shape (Square), Color (Black). **Answer Choice A is WRONG.

** Read the way Arrow is pointed (Left to Right). **Answer Choice C is WRONG.**

FUNDAMENTAL
CONCEPTS

Figures with NO (Zero) Sides

Figures with ONE Side

Figures with TWO Sides

   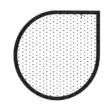

FUNDAMENTAL CONCEPTS

Figures with THREE Sides

3-sides of
Equal Length

2-sides of
Equal Length

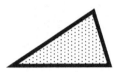

NO-sides of
Equal Length

Figures with THREE Sides

RIGHT Angle
Triangle

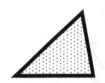

ACUTE Angle
Triangle

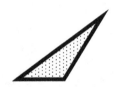

OBTUSE Angle
Triangle

Figures with FOUR Sides

   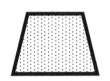

12

Figures with FOUR Sides

 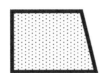  

Figures with FIVE Sides

  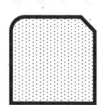 

Figures with SIX Sides

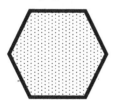   

Figures with SEVEN Sides

Figures with EIGHT Sides

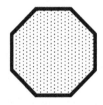 

Figures with NINE Sides

Figures with TEN Sides

Figures with TWELVE Sides

POSITION

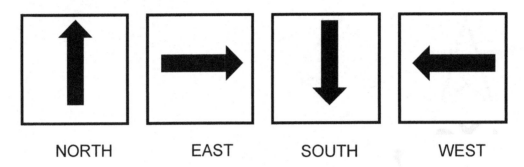

NORTH   EAST   SOUTH   WEST

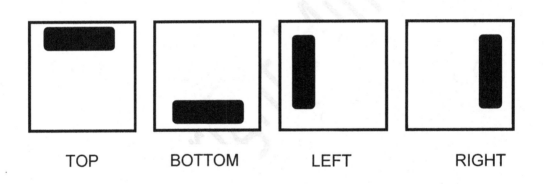

TOP   BOTTOM   LEFT   RIGHT

CORNER#1   CORNER#2   CORNER#3   CORNER#4

Rotation

CLOCK-WISE

COUNTER CLOCK-WISE

COLOR

FILL

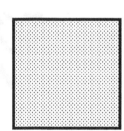

PATTERN

OUTLINE

ANALOGY

CHANGE
Number of Sides

ADD ONE or MORE SIDES

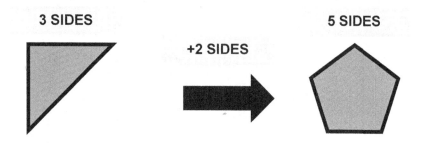

3 SIDES   +2 SIDES   5 SIDES

DOUBLE the NUMBER OF SIDES

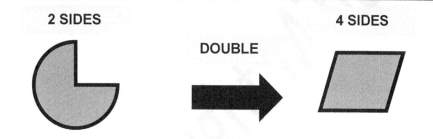

2 SIDES   DOUBLE   4 SIDES

SUBTRACT ONE or MORE SIDES

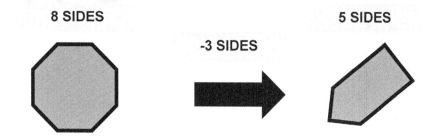

8 SIDES   -3 SIDES   5 SIDES

HALF the NUMBER OF SIDES

10 SIDES   **5 SIDES**

HALF

ADD or DOUBLE
NUMBER OF SIDES

4 SIDES   DOUBLE # of SIDES   **8 SIDES**

(or) +4

SUBTRACT or HALF
NUMBER OF SIDES

HALF # of SIDES

8 SIDES   (or) -4   **4 SIDES**

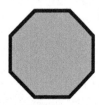 

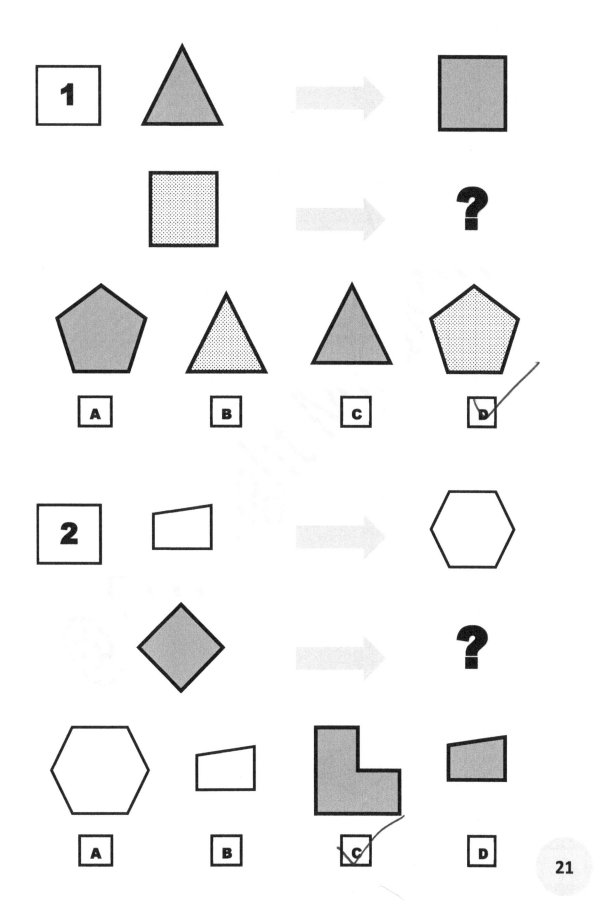

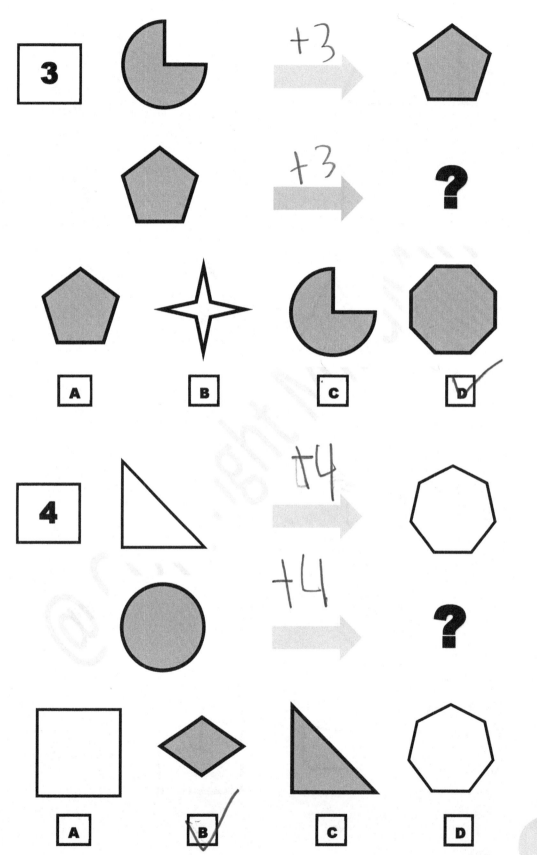

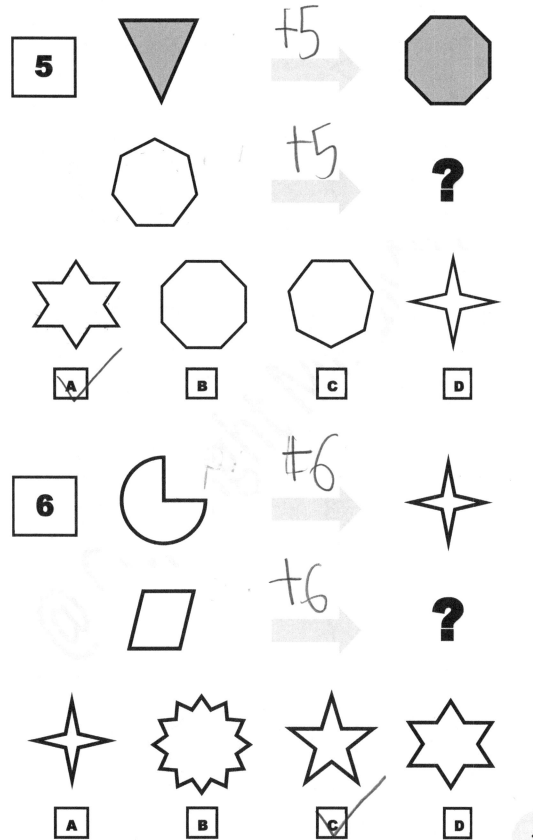

+5

+5

5

A B C D

+6

+6

6

A B C D

23

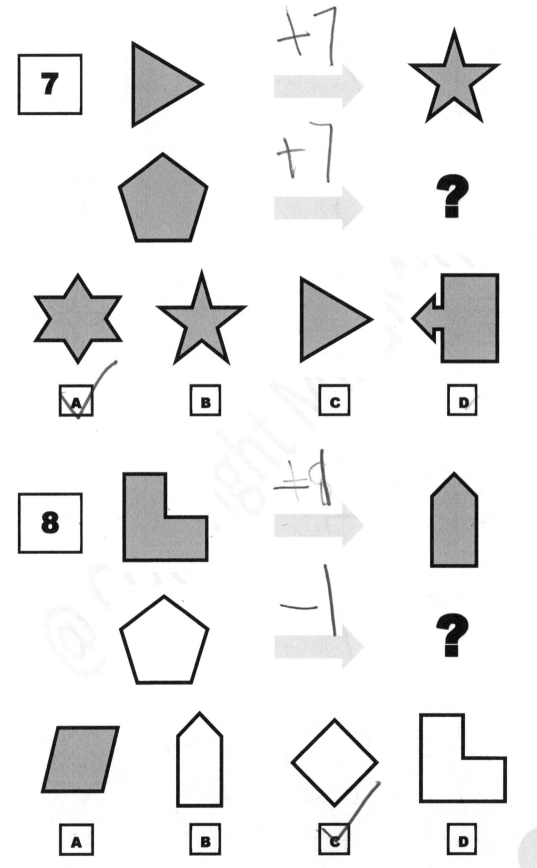

7

A

8

A   B   C   D

24

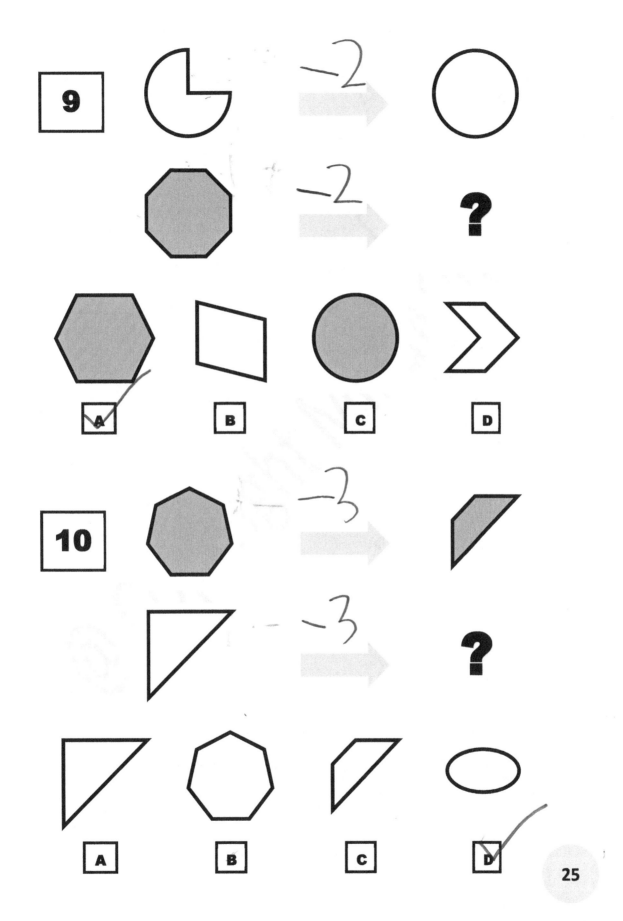

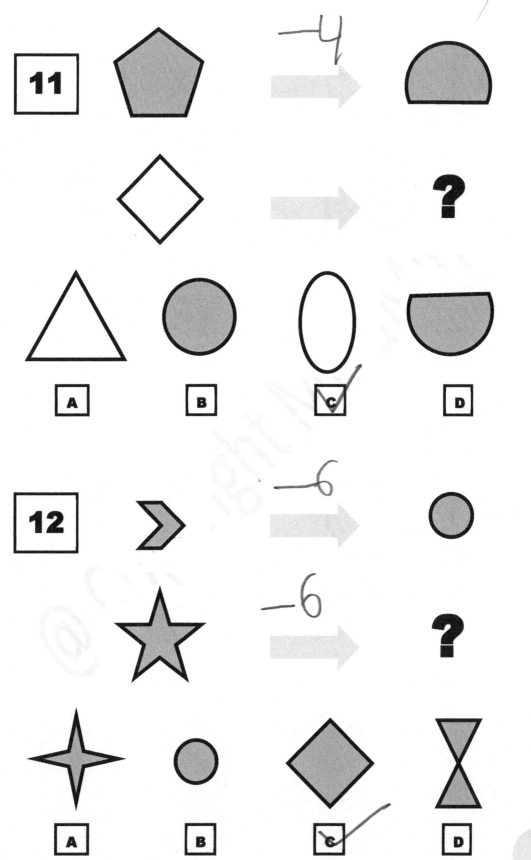

11

12

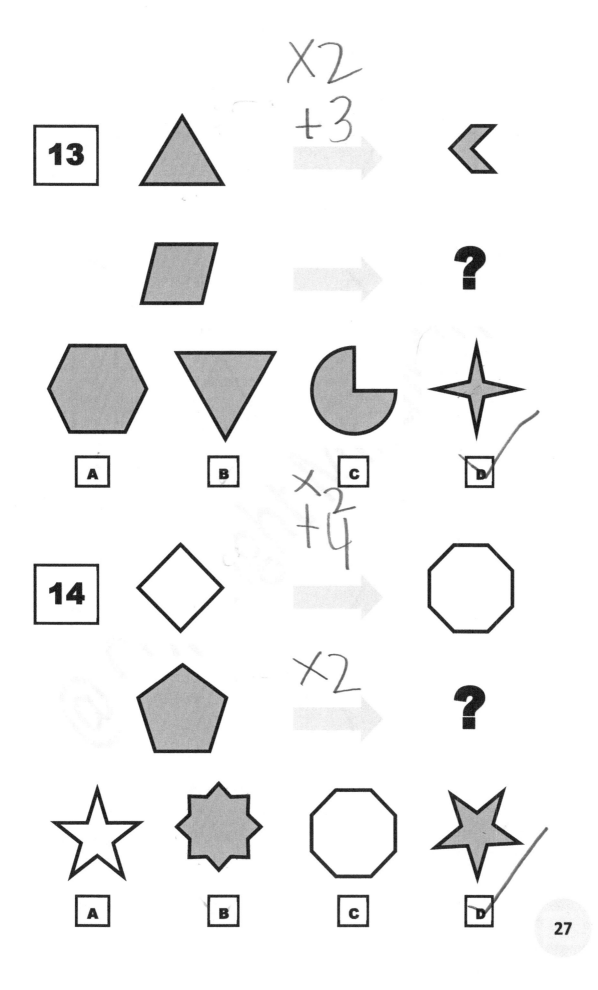

×2
+3

13

×2
+4

14

×2

27

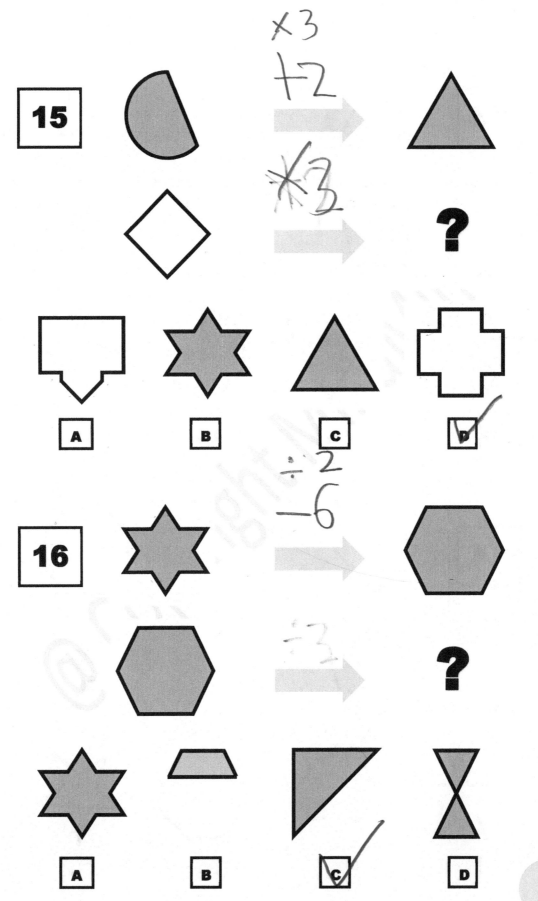

15

×3
+2
×3

A   B   C   D

÷2
−6

16

×3

A   B   C   D

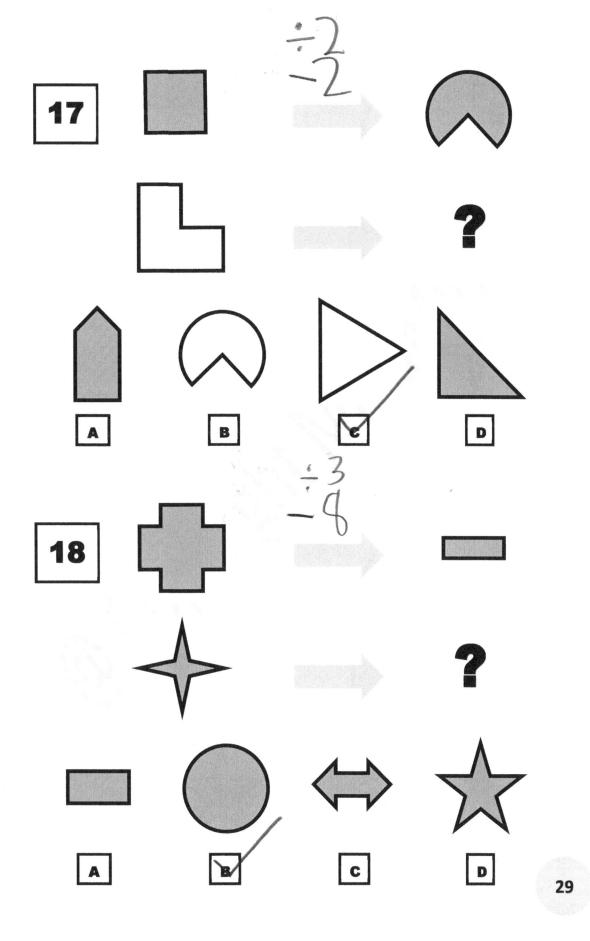

17

18

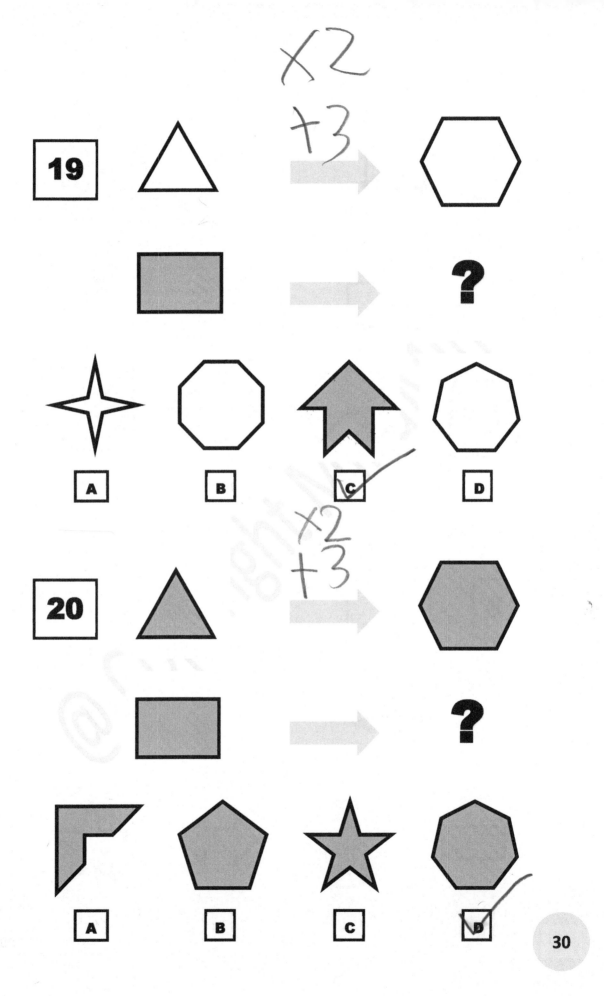

19

×2
+3

| A | B | C | D |

20

×2
+3

| A | B | C | D |

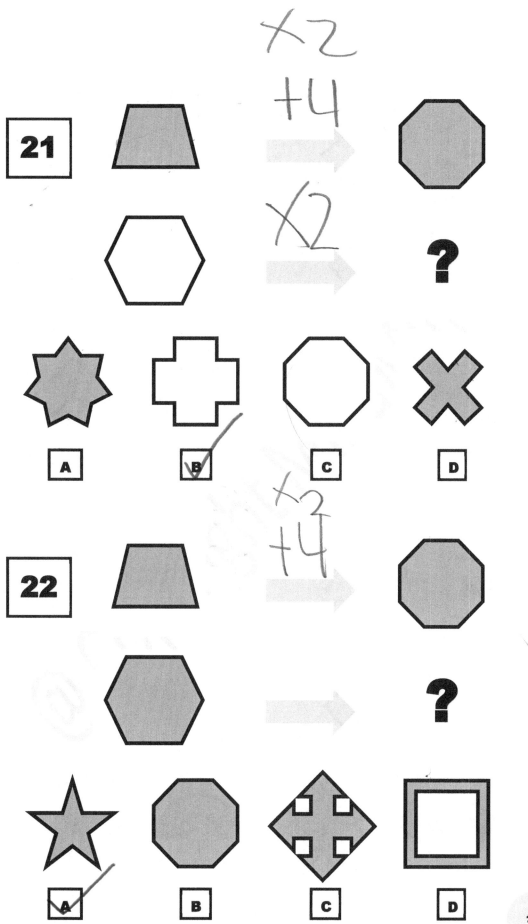

21

×2
+4

×2

A   B   C   D

×2
+4

22

A   B   C   D

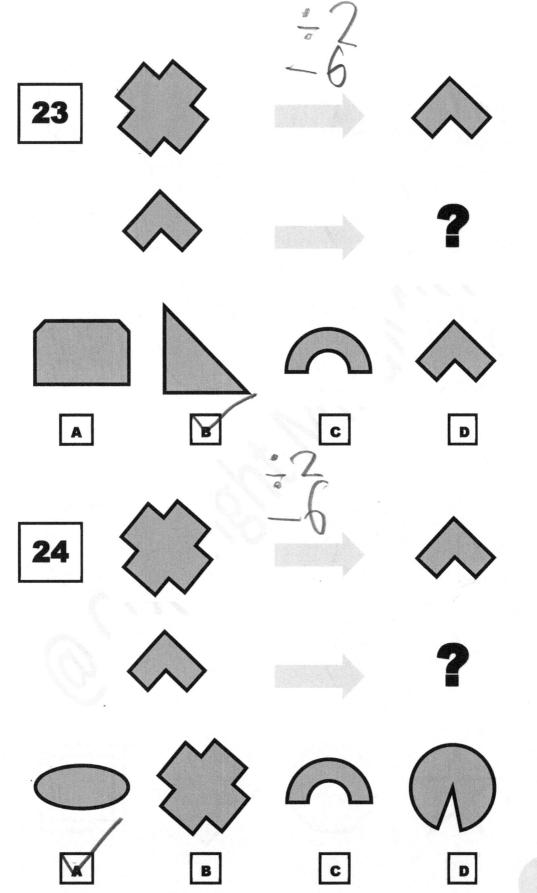

23

A   B   C   D

24

A   B   C   D

25

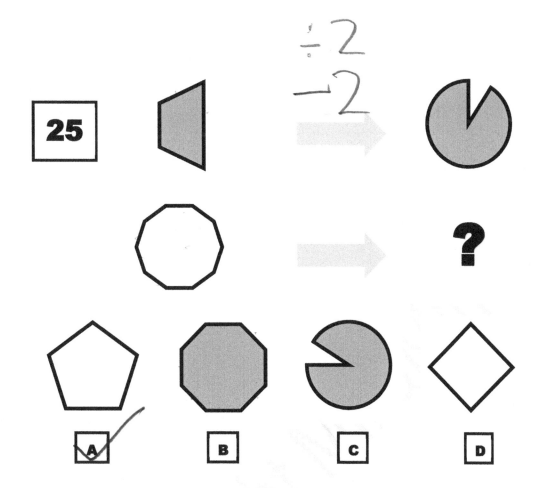

÷2

A   B   C   D

ANALOGY

CHANGE

COLOR

Change Color

Change Color

To BLACK

Change Pattern

Change Pattern

To

Horizontal Lines

Change OUTLINE

Change Outline

To

Dotted Lines

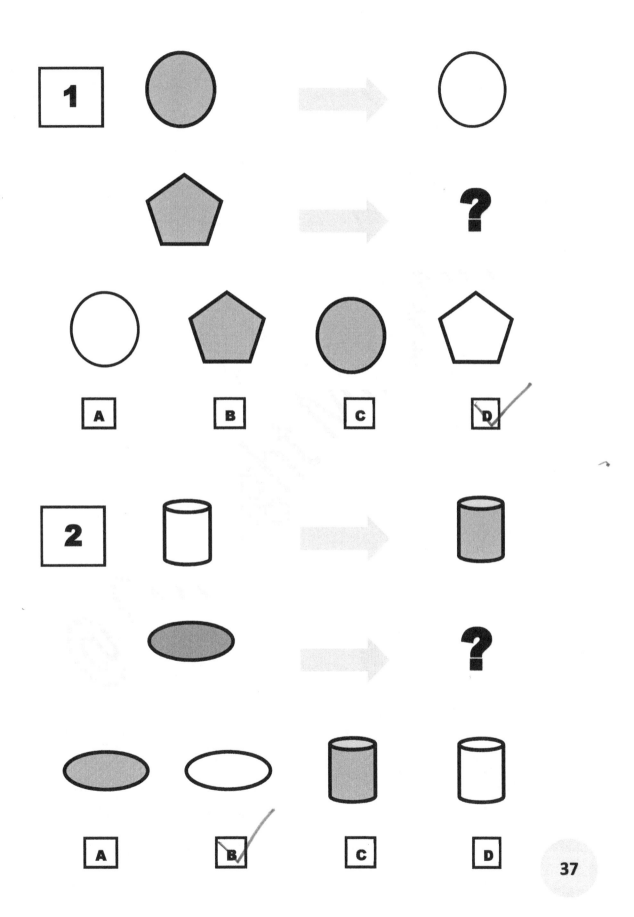

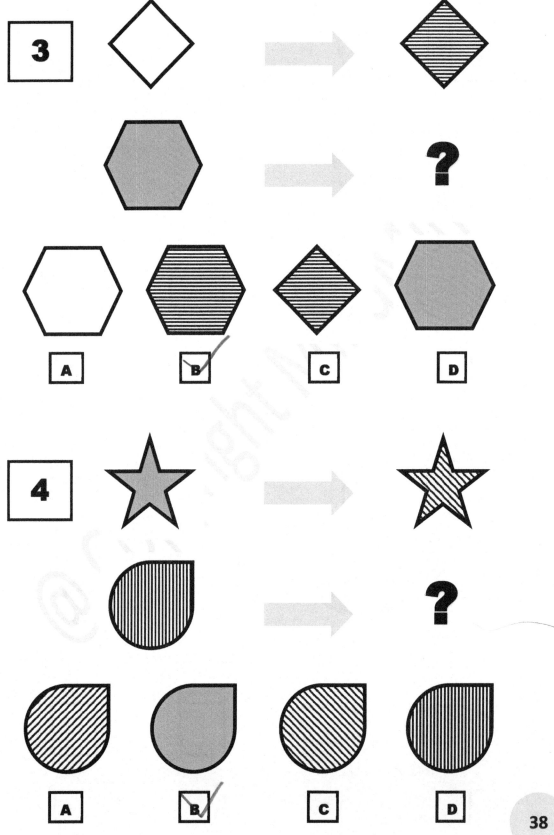

38

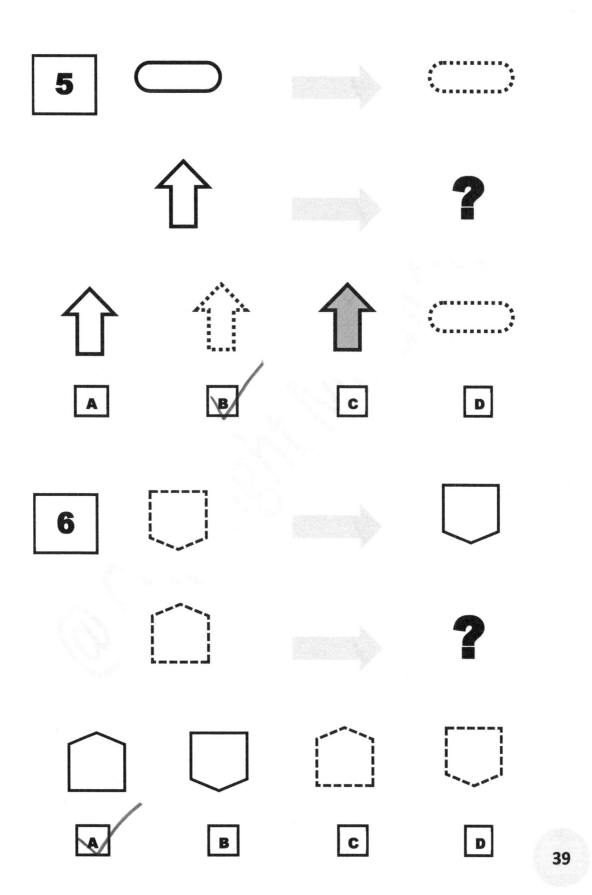

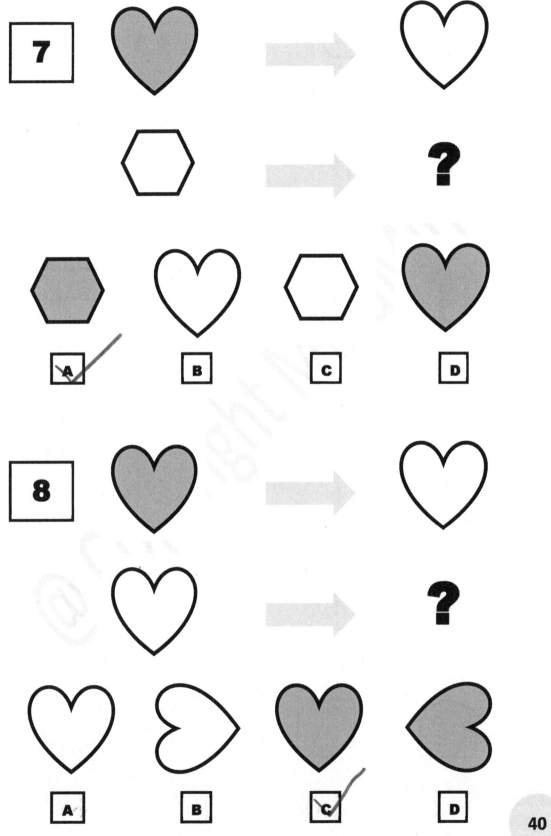

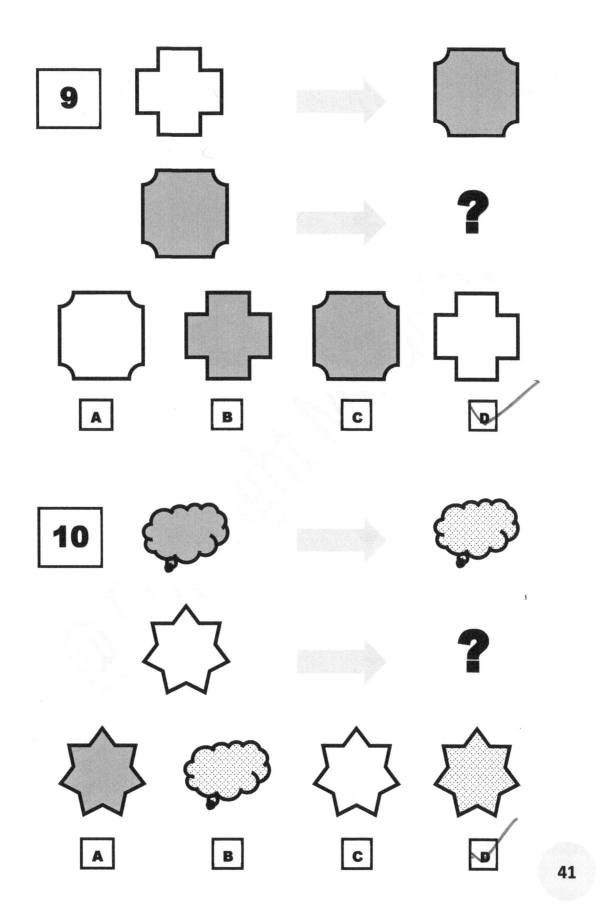

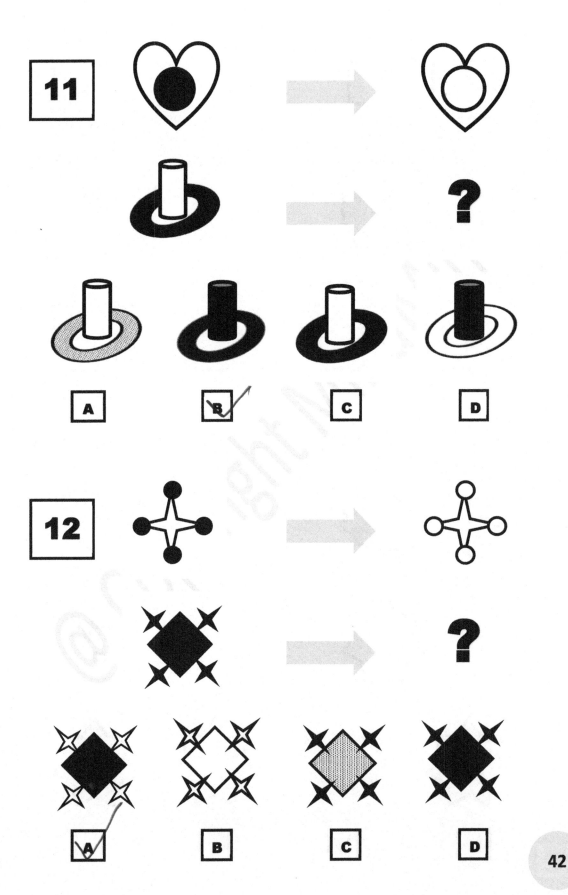

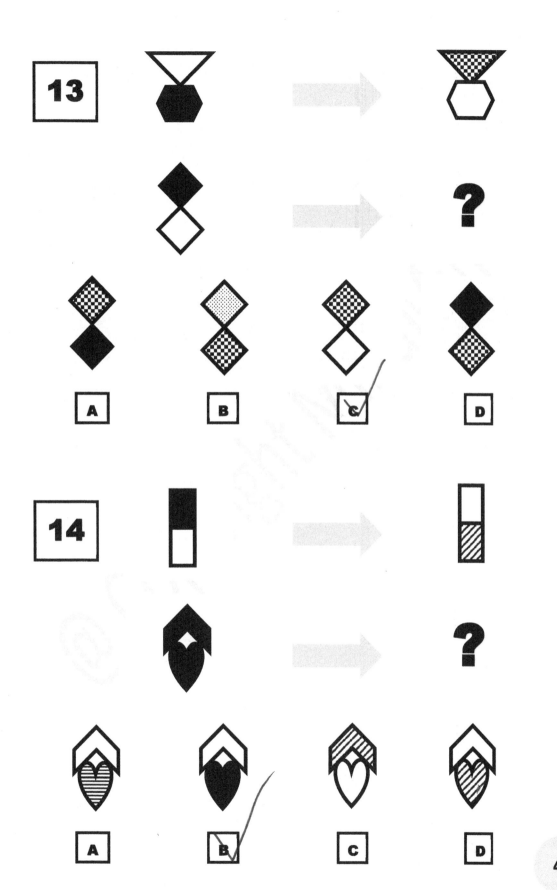

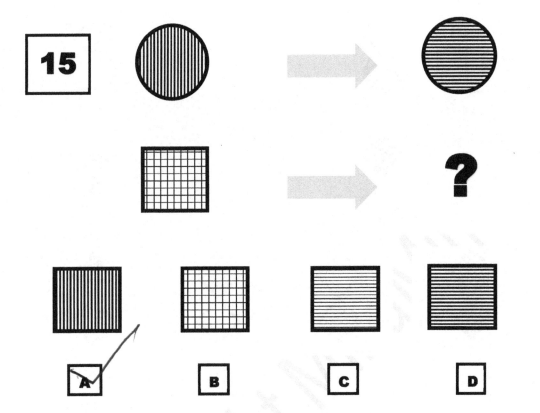

ANALOGY

CHANGE
Size

Change Size - Make BIG
(Increase LENGTH & WIDTH)

Make Big

Change Size – Make SMALL
(Decrease LENGTH & WIDTH)

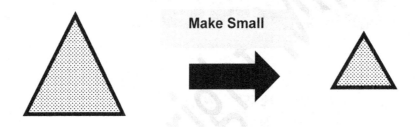

Make Small

Change Size
Increase Length (or Base) ONLY

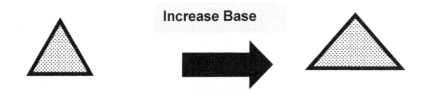

Increase Base

Change Size

Increase HEIGHT ONLY

Increase Height

Change Size

Decrease Length (or Base) ONLY

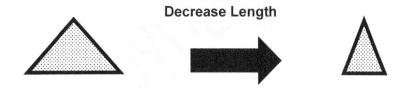

Decrease Length

Change Size

Decrease HEIGHT ONLY

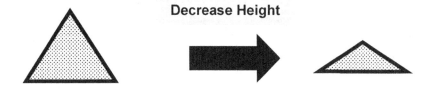

Decrease Height

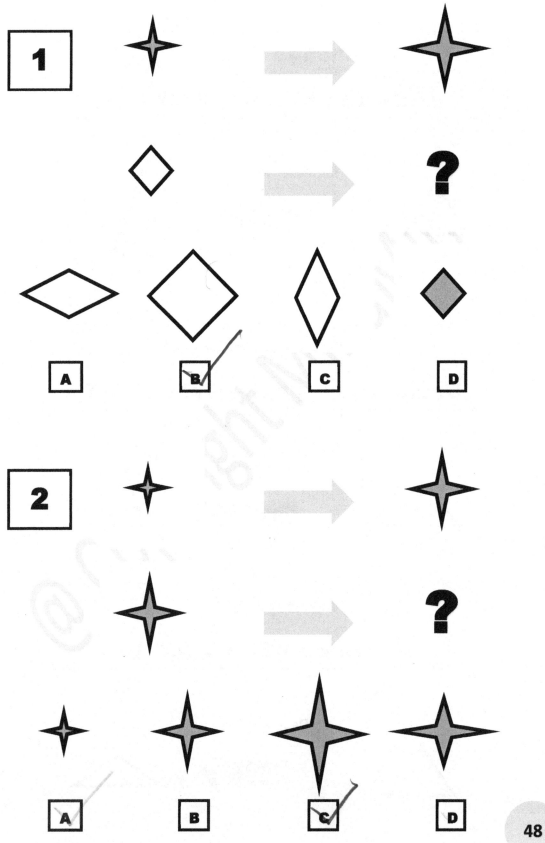

48

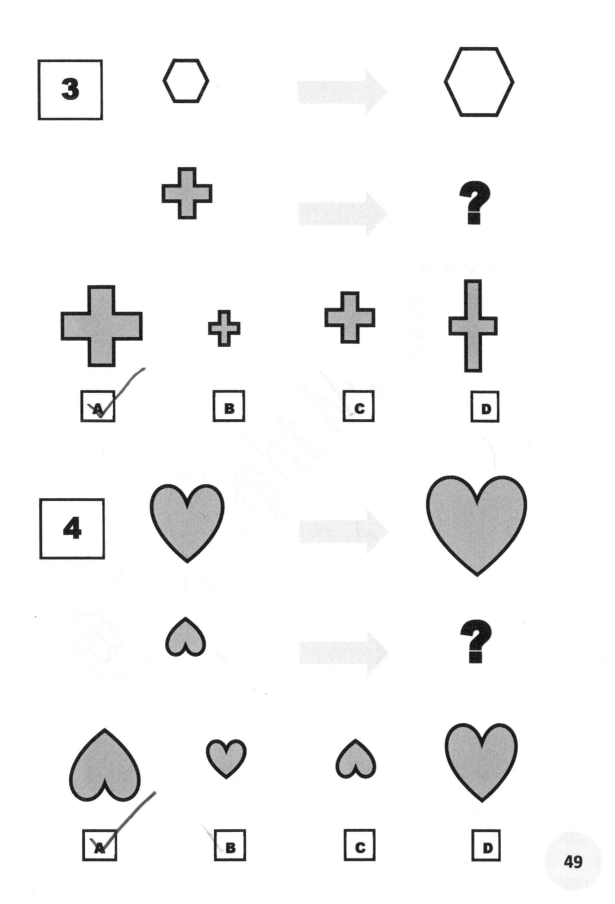

3

4

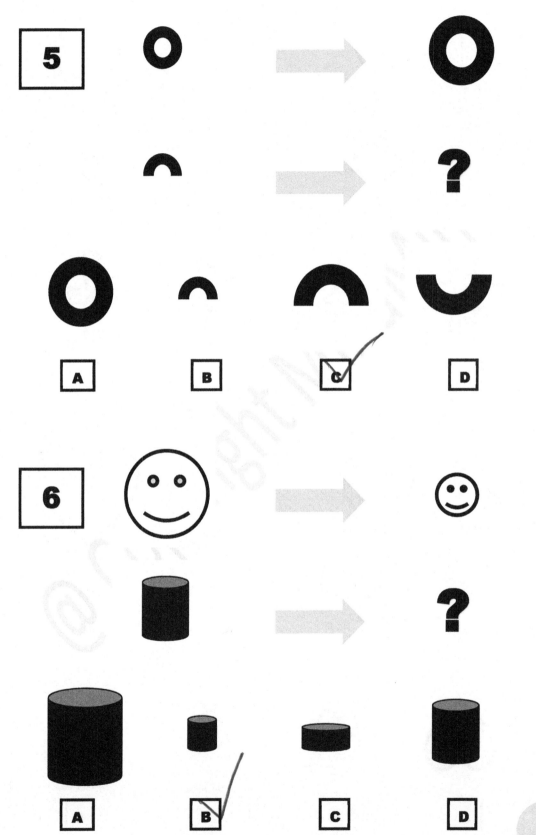

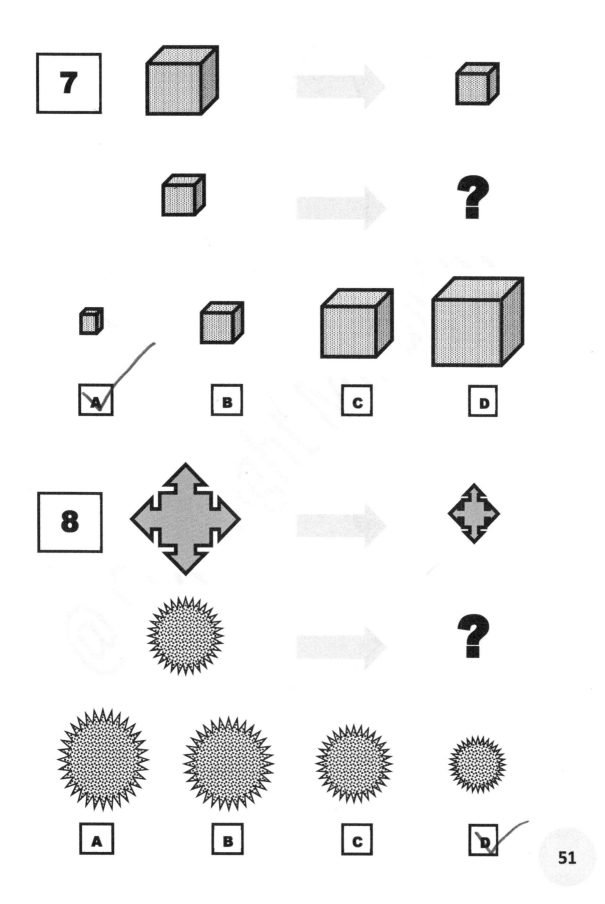

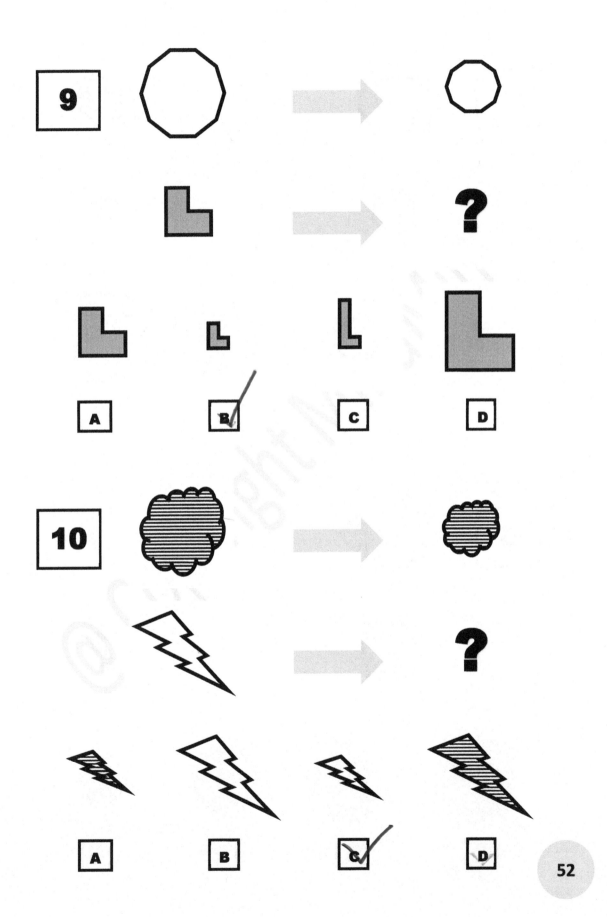

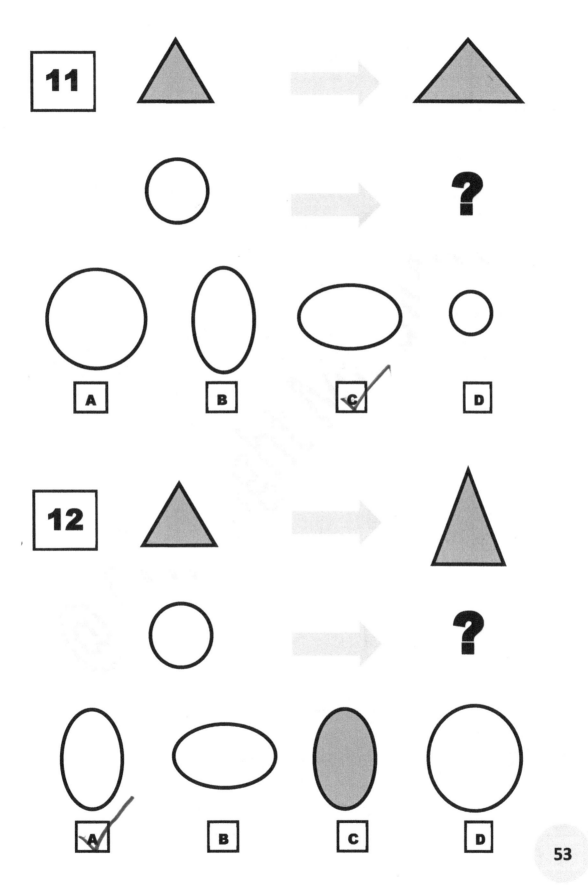

11

A   B   C   D

12

A   B   C   D

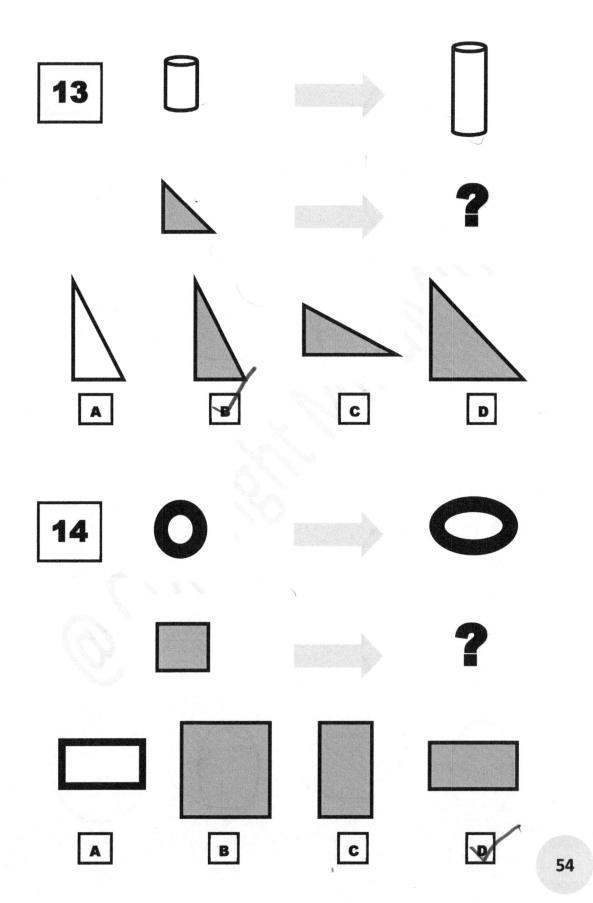

13

A B C D

14

A B C D

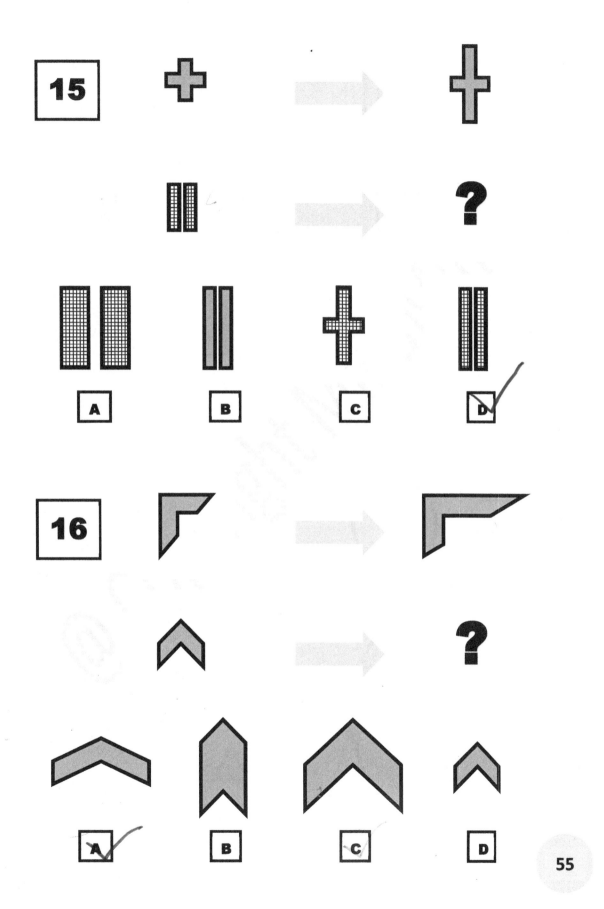

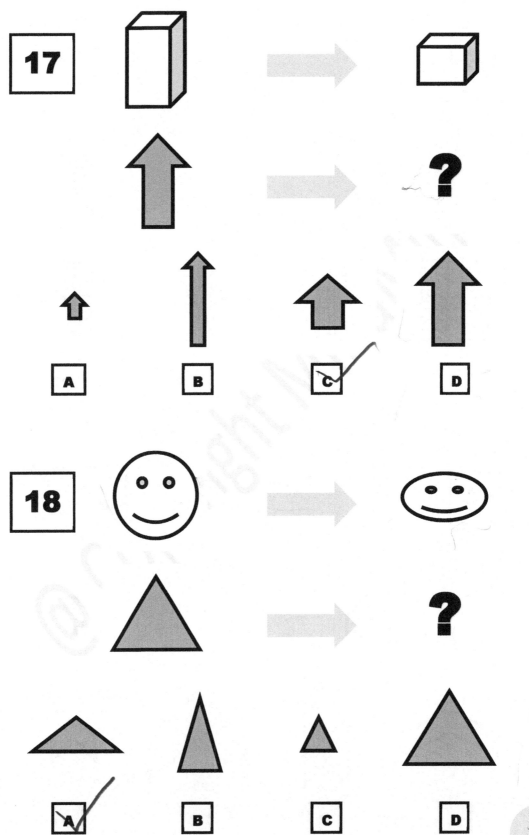

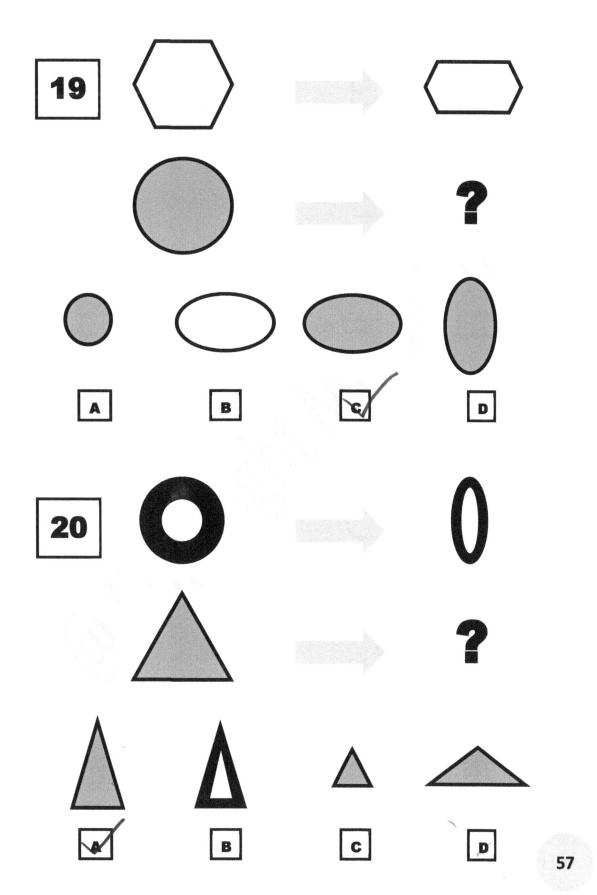

19

A

B

C

D

20

A

B

C

D

57

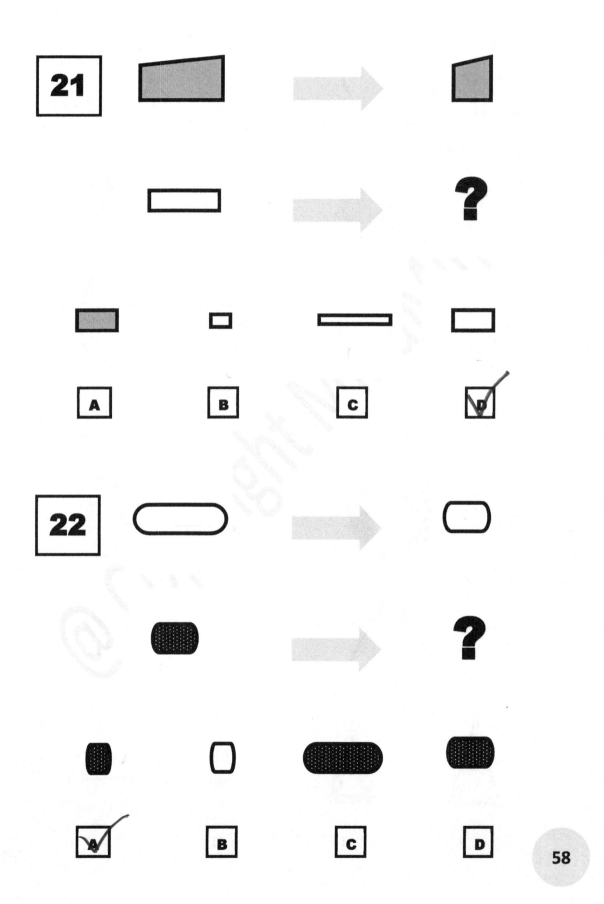

21

A B C D

22

A B C D

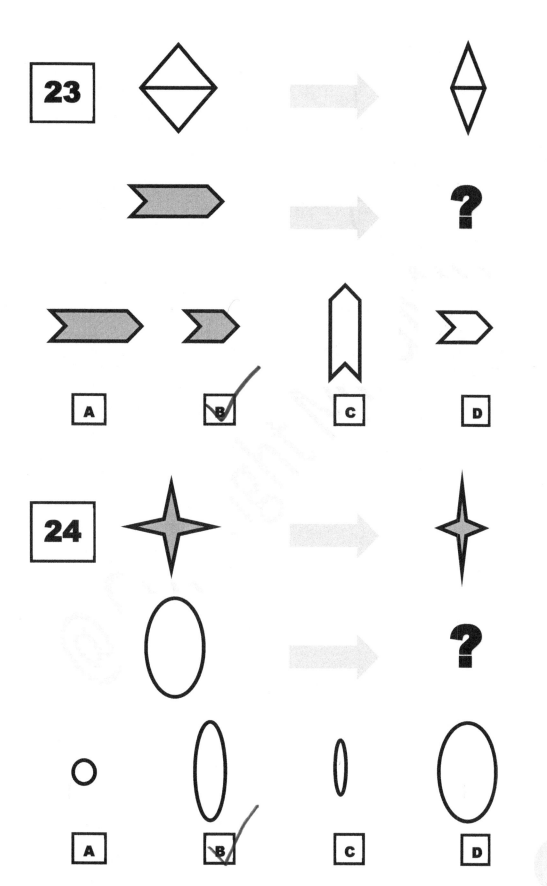

23

A

B

C

D

24

A

B

C

D

25

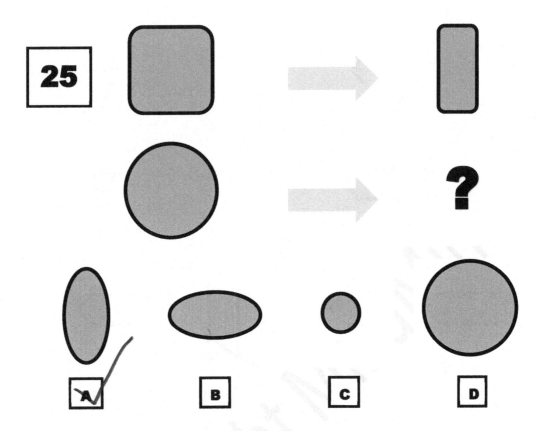

ANALOGY

FLIP
(REFLECTION)

FLIP UPSIDE DOWN

FLIP

UPSIDE DOWN

FLIP SIDEWAYS

FLIP

SIDEWAYS

FLIP UPSIDE DOWN

FLIP

UPSIDE DOWN

Note: Same shape results when flipped upside down

FLIP SIDEWAYS

FLIP

SIDEWAYS

Note: Same shape results when flipped sideways

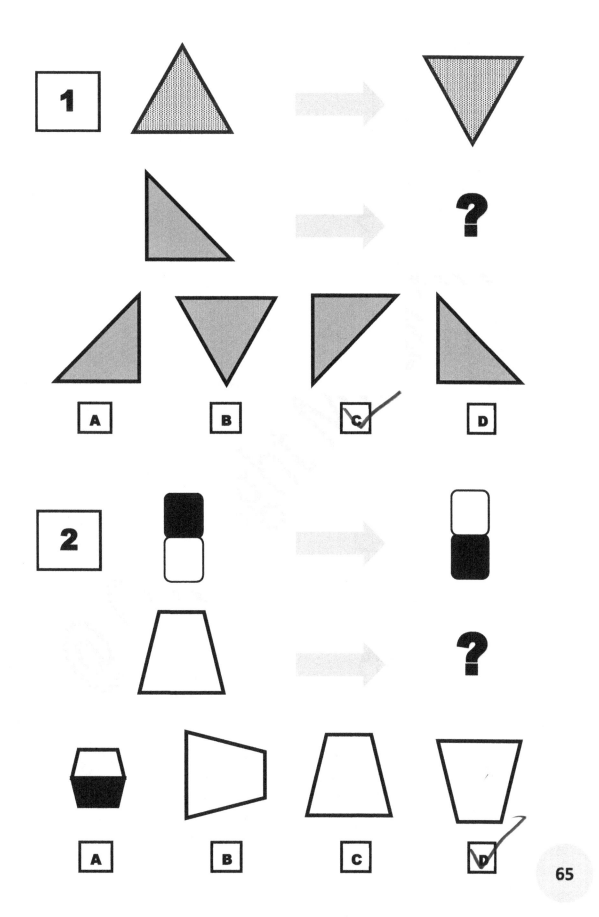

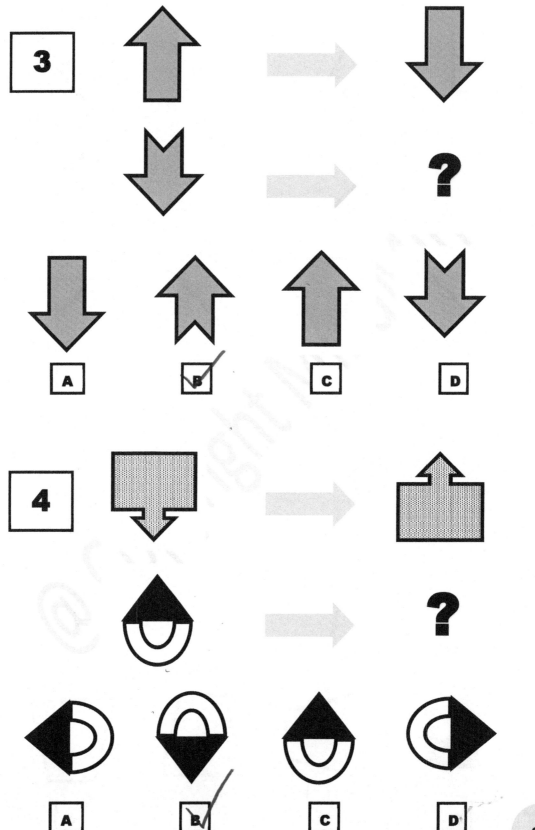

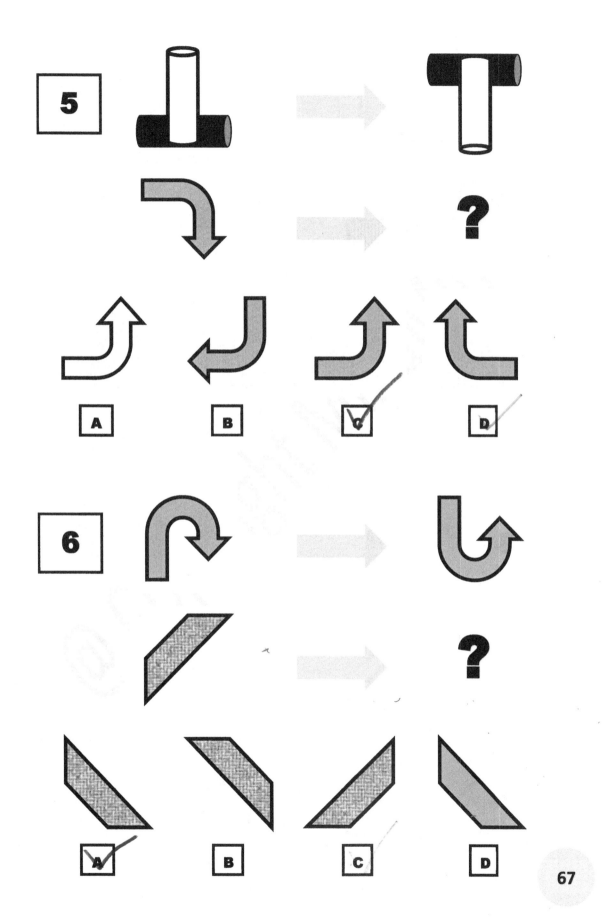

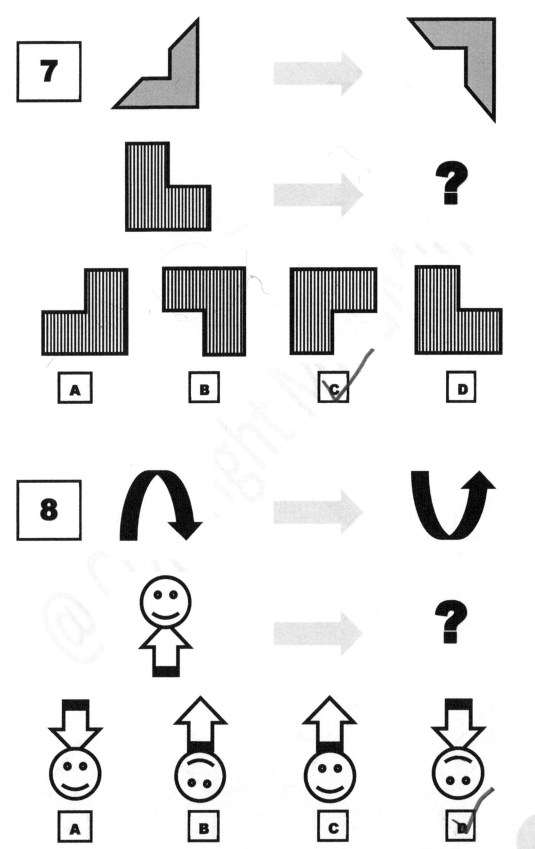

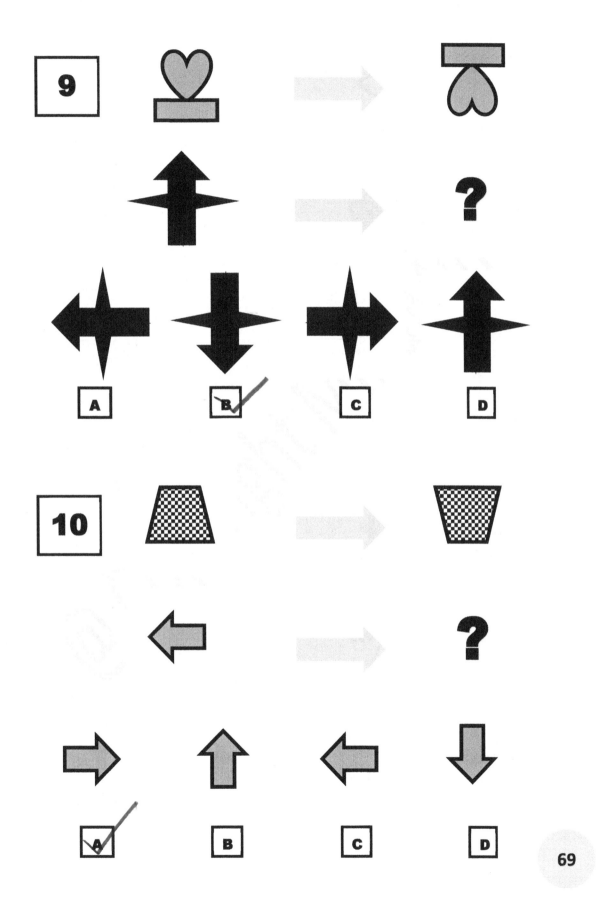

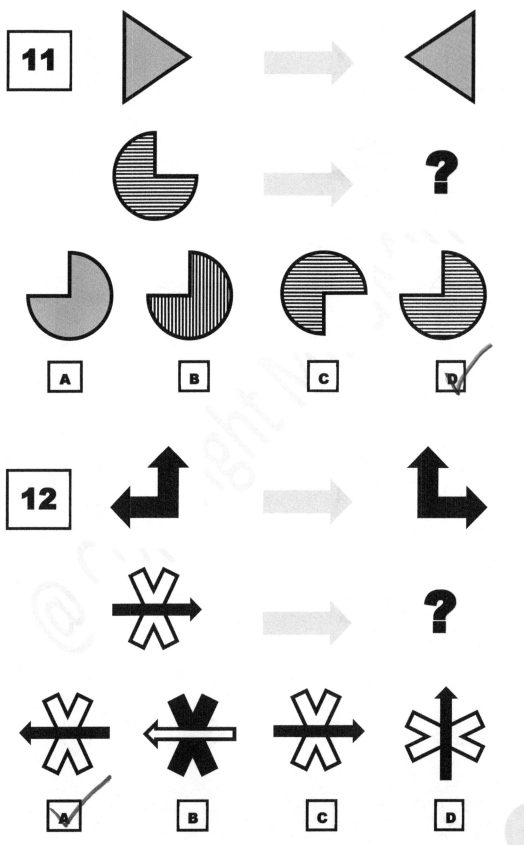

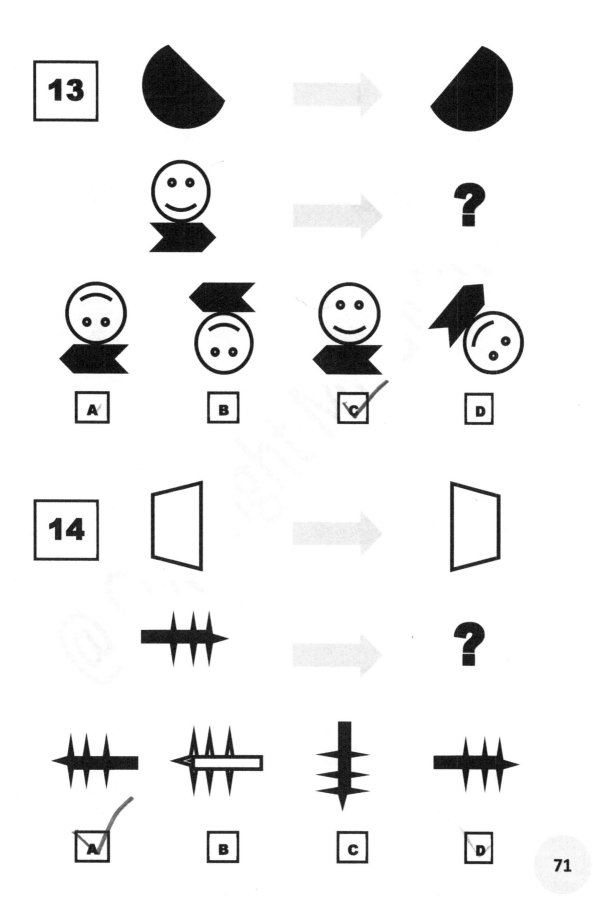

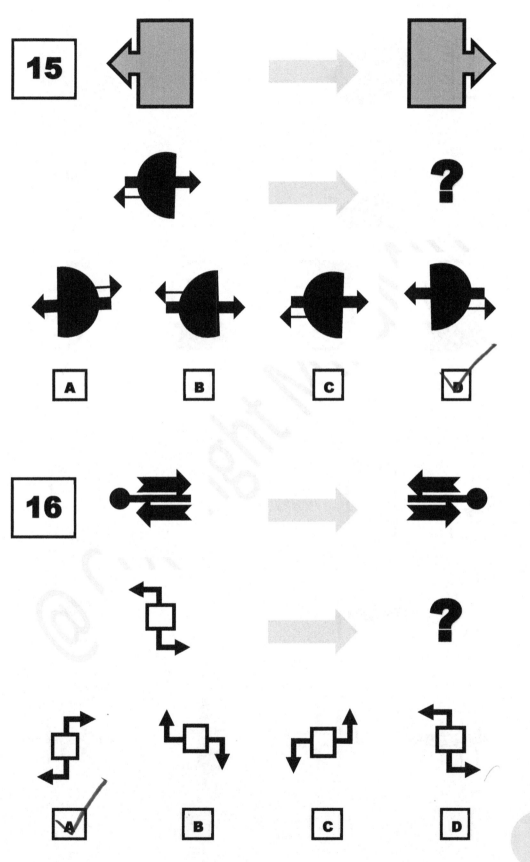

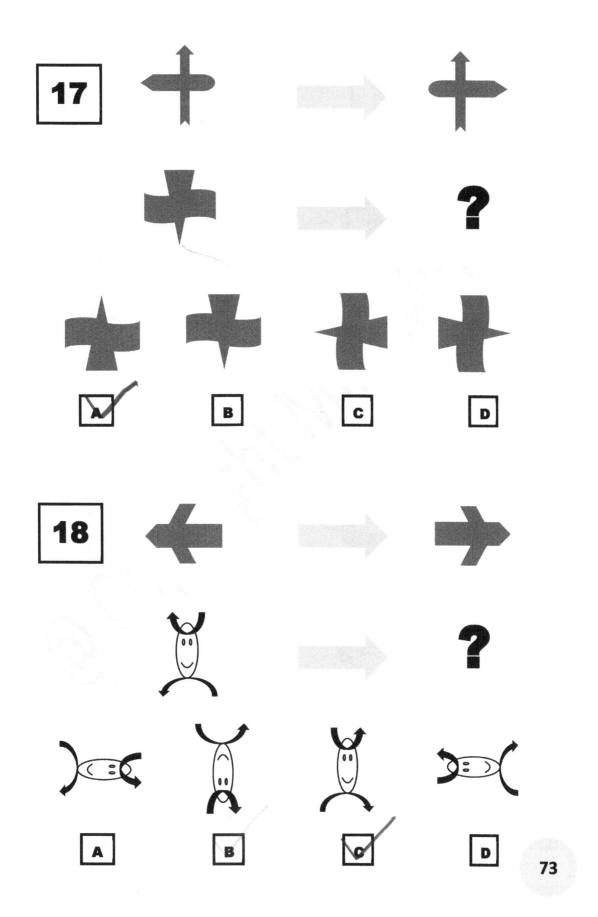

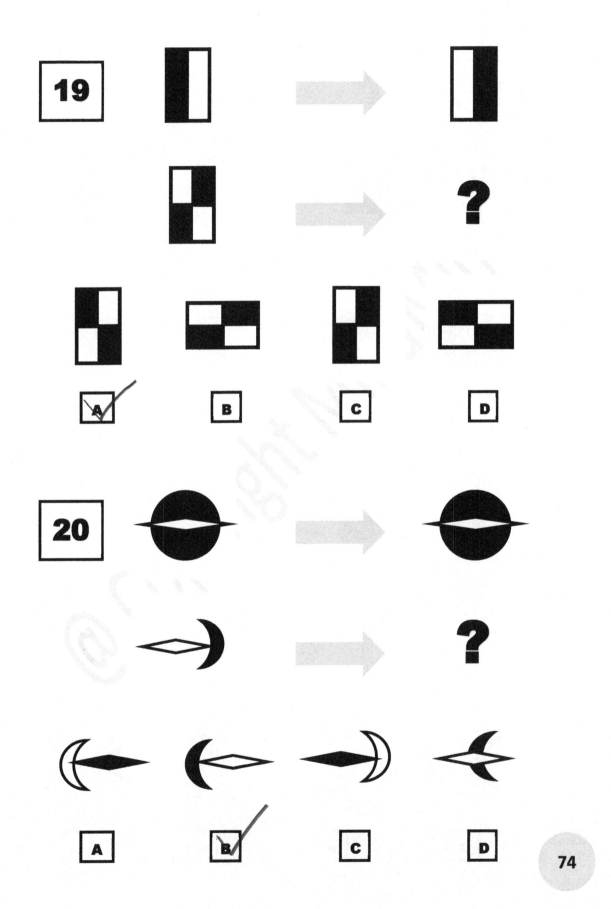

ANALOGY

CUT FIGURE

CUT TOP

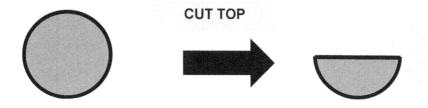

CUT TOP

CUT BOTTOM

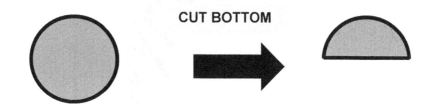

CUT BOTTOM

CUT LEFT

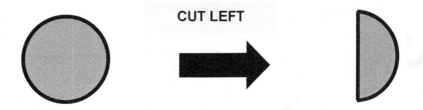

CUT LEFT

CUT RIGHT

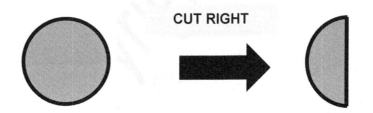

CUT RIGHT

78

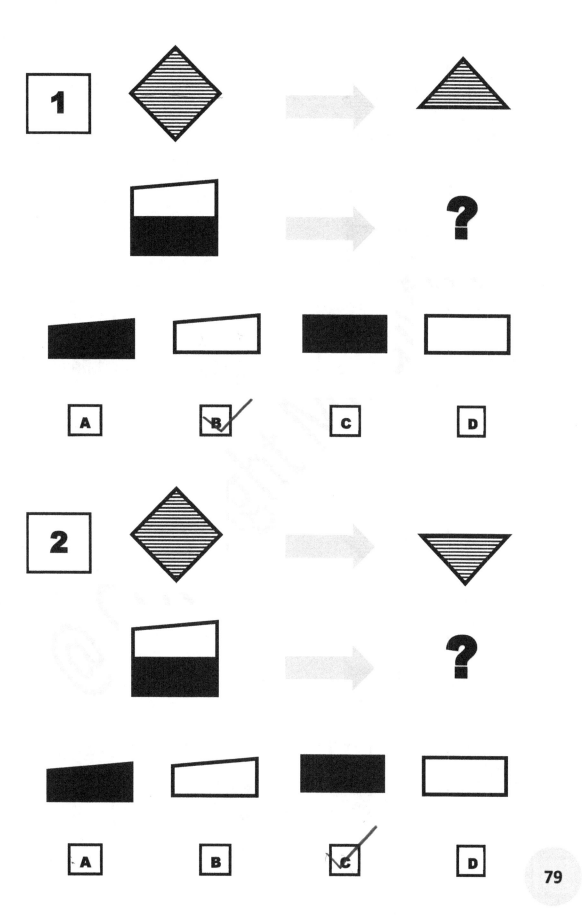

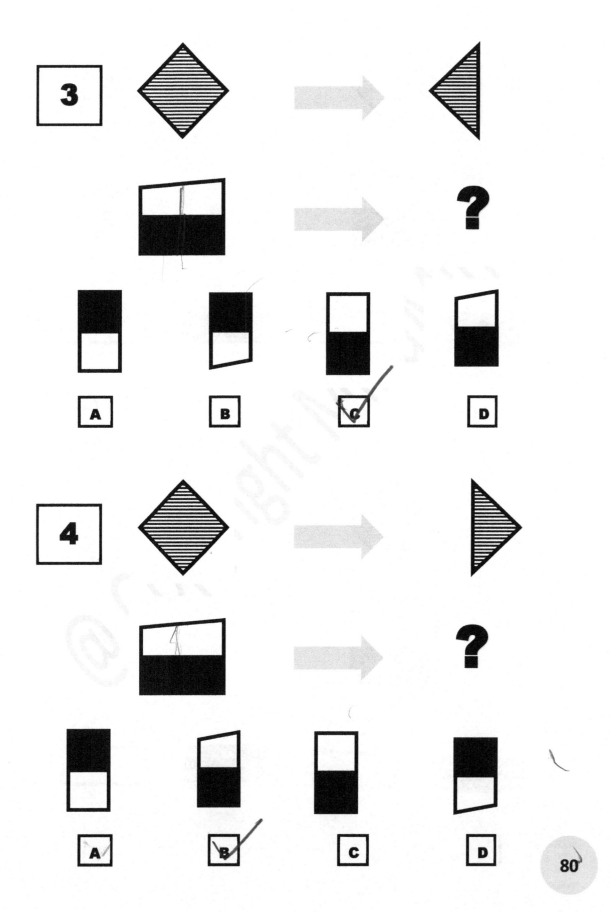

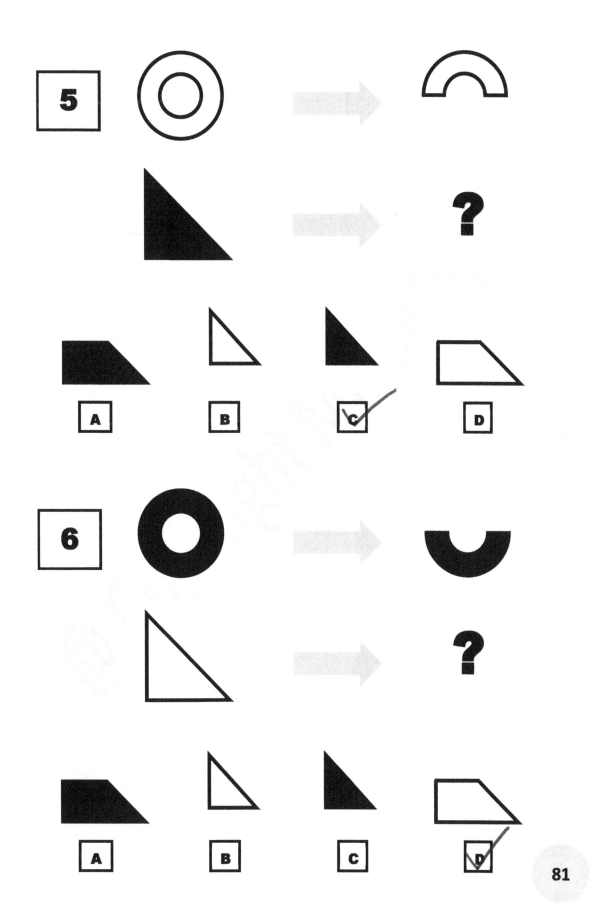

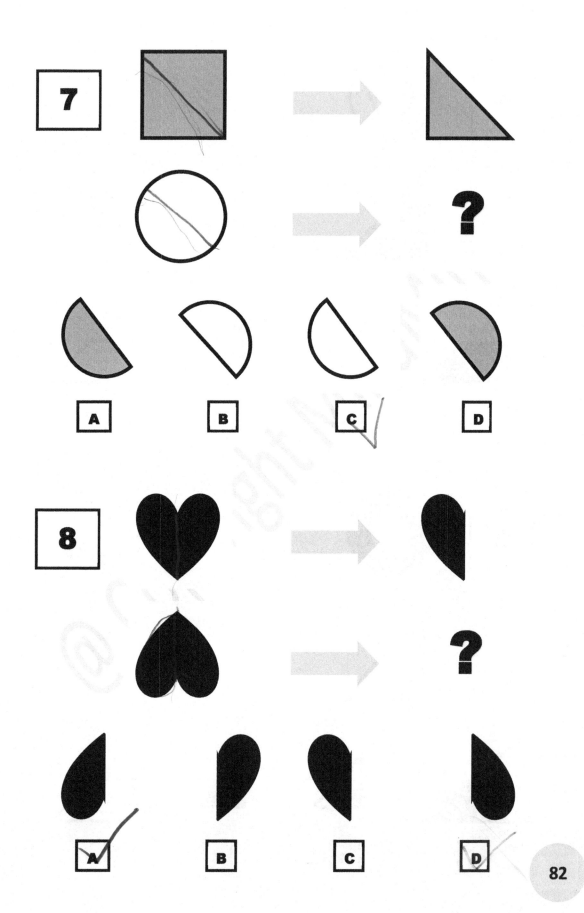

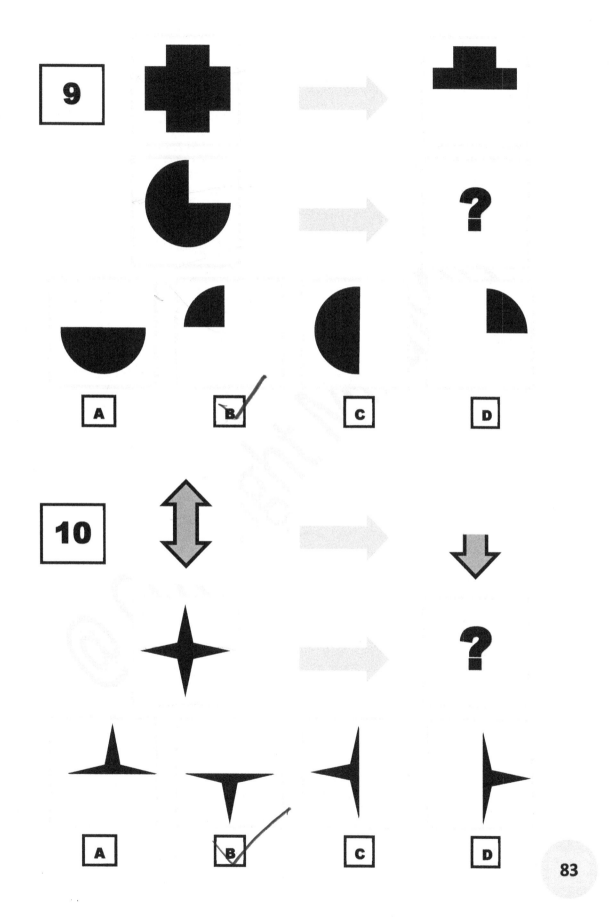

83

ANALOGY

ADD (or) REMOVE A Figure

ADD a FIGURE

Add a Figure

Inside

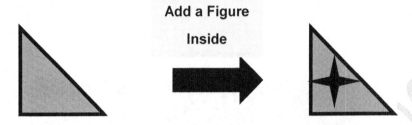

ADD SAME FIGURE

Add SAME Figure

Inside

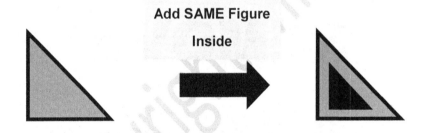

ADD a FIGURE

Add a Figure

OUTSIDE

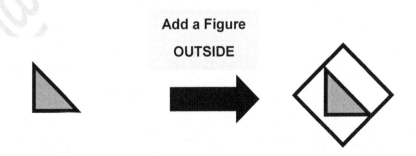

REMOVE a FIGURE

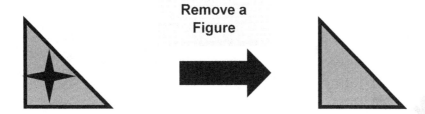

Remove a Figure

REMOVE a Side

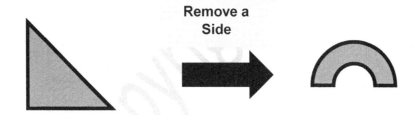

Remove a Side

87

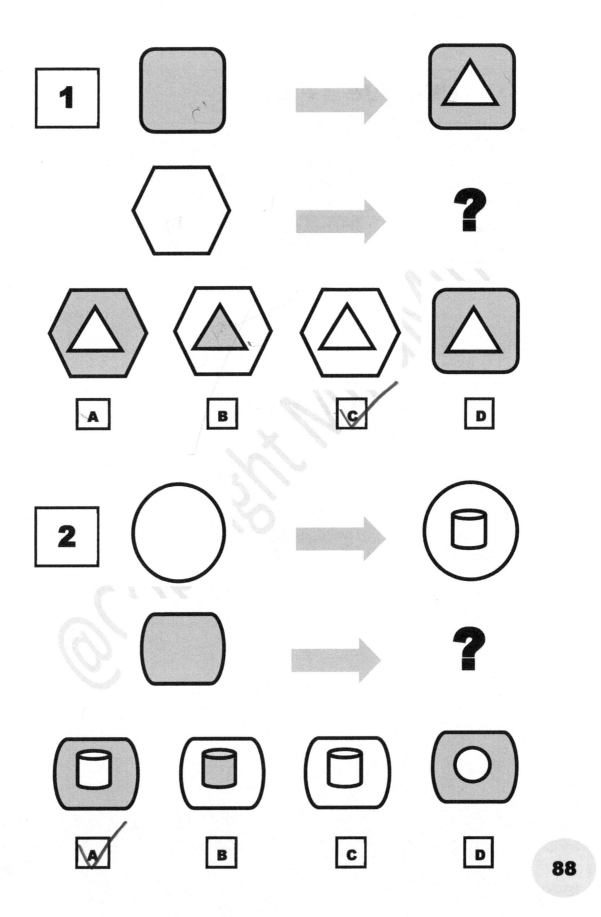

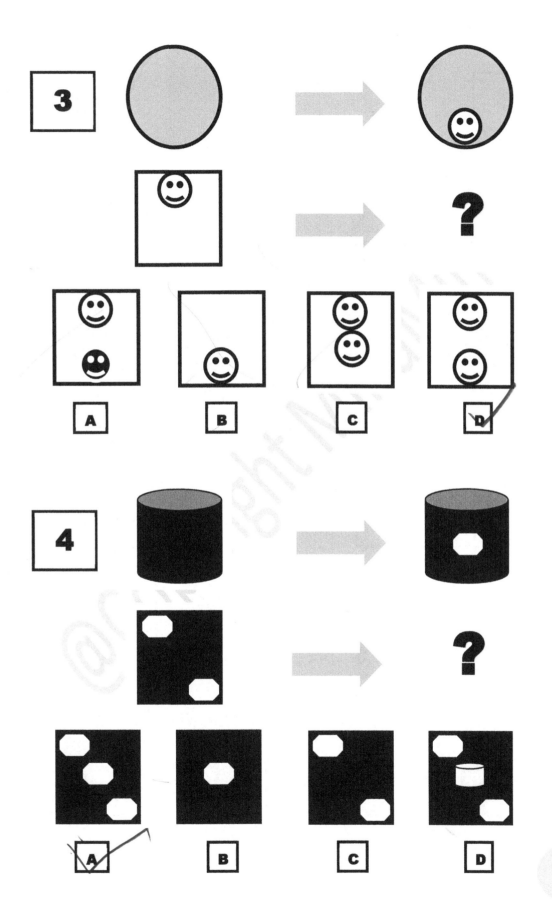

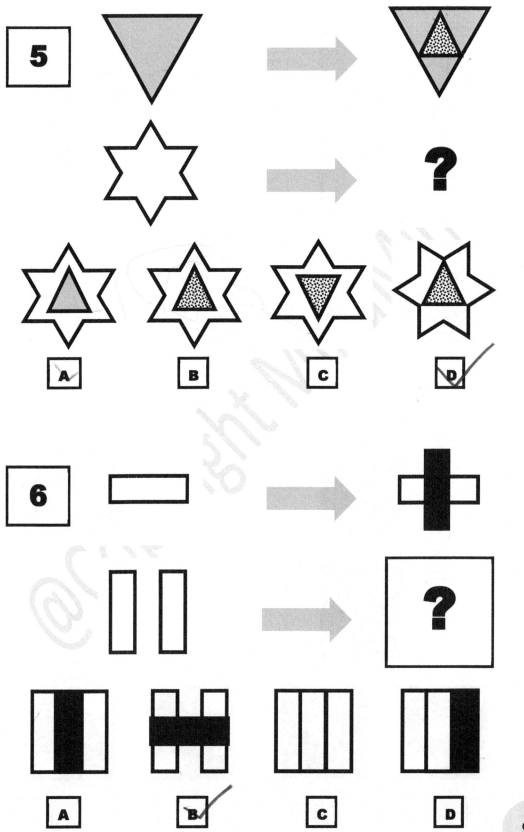

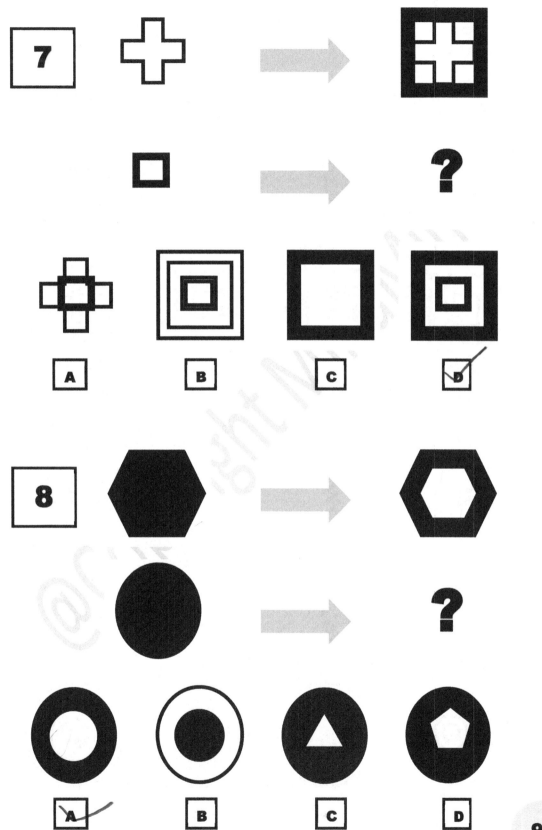

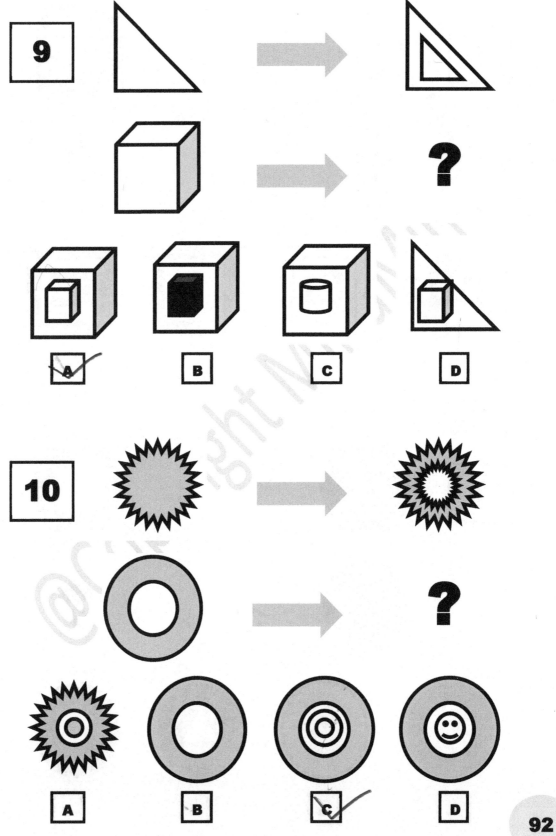

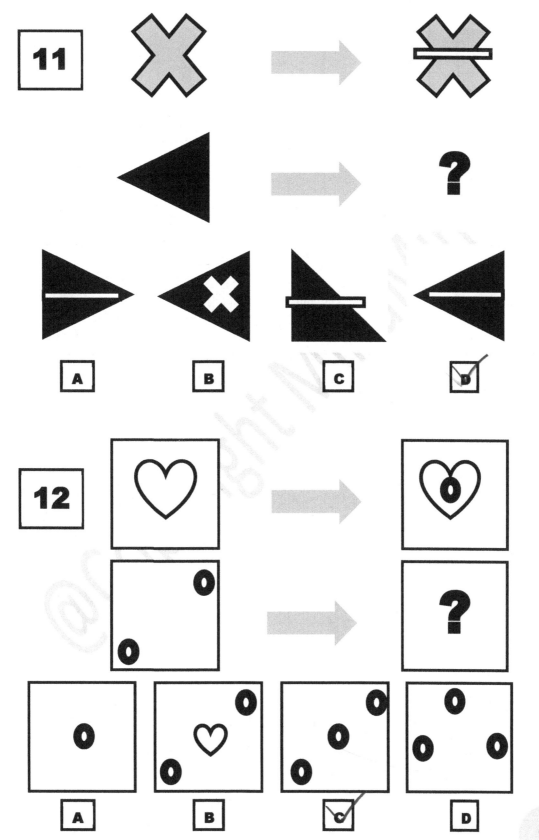

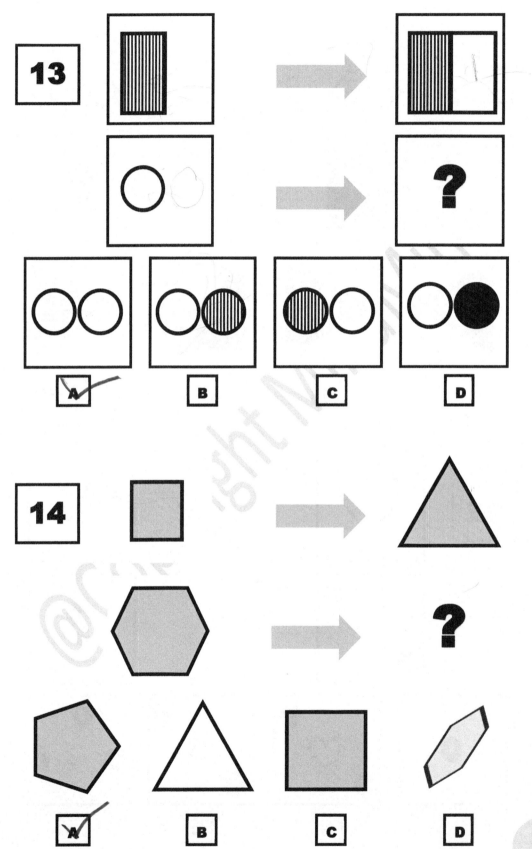

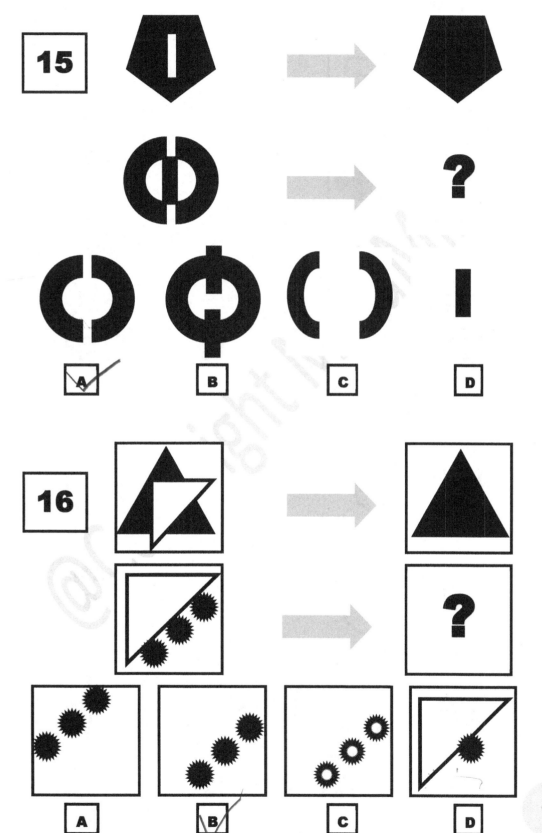

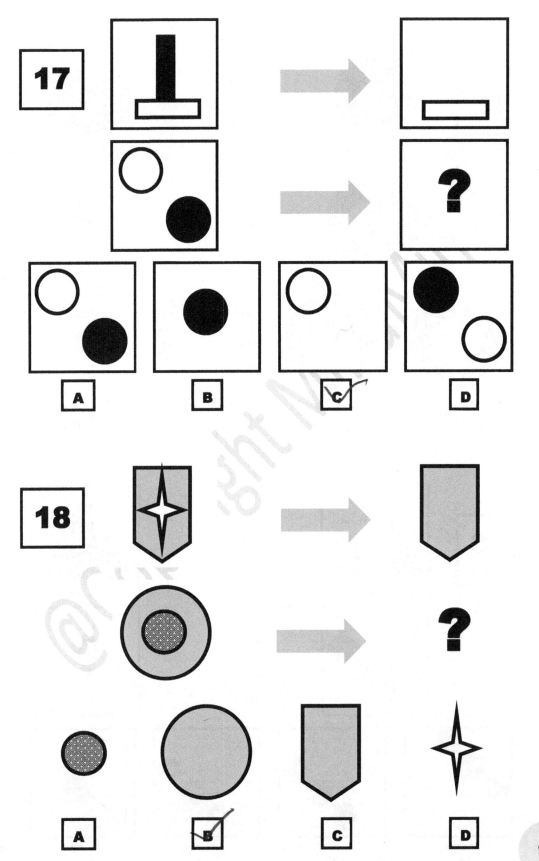

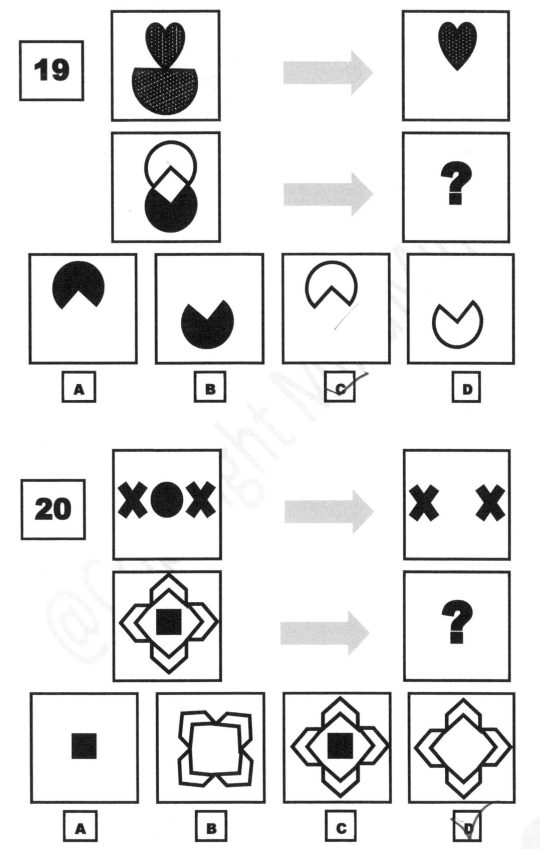

ANALOGY

MOVE

MOVE FIGURE
ALL THE WAY TO RIGHT

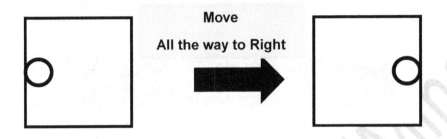

MOVE FIGURE
ALL THE WAY TO LEFT

MOVE FIGURE
ALL THE WAY TO UP

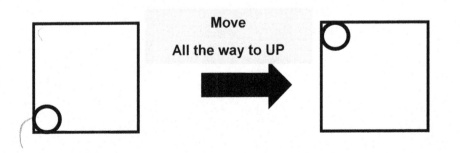

MOVE FIGURE
ALL THE WAY TO DOWN

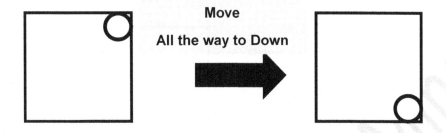

MOVE FIGURE
HALF WAY TO LEFT

MOVE FIGURE
HALF WAY TO RIGHT

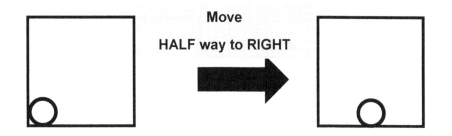

MOVE FIGURE
HALF WAY TO UP

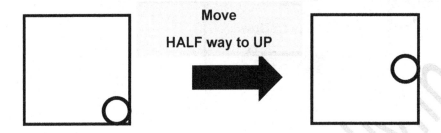

Move
HALF way to UP

MOVE FIGURE
HALF WAY TO DOWN

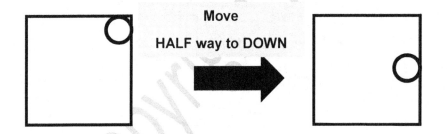

Move
HALF way to DOWN

MOVE FIGURE
HALF WAY TO UP

Move
HALF way to UP

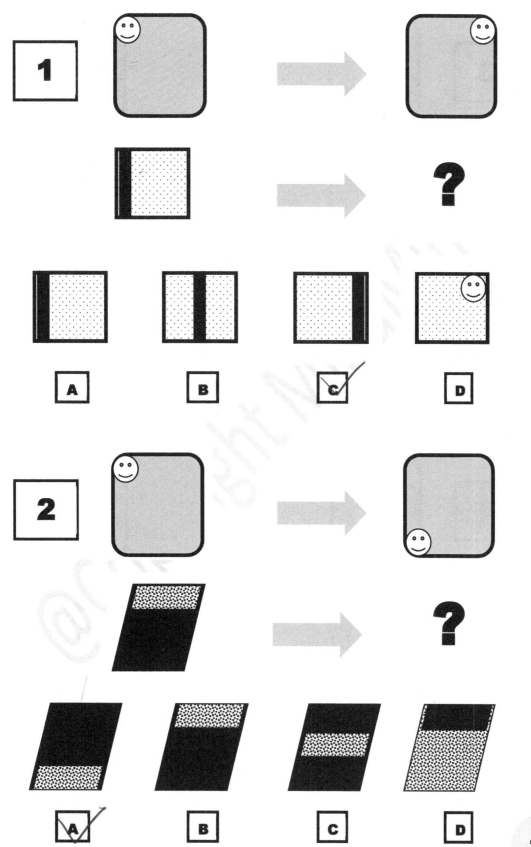

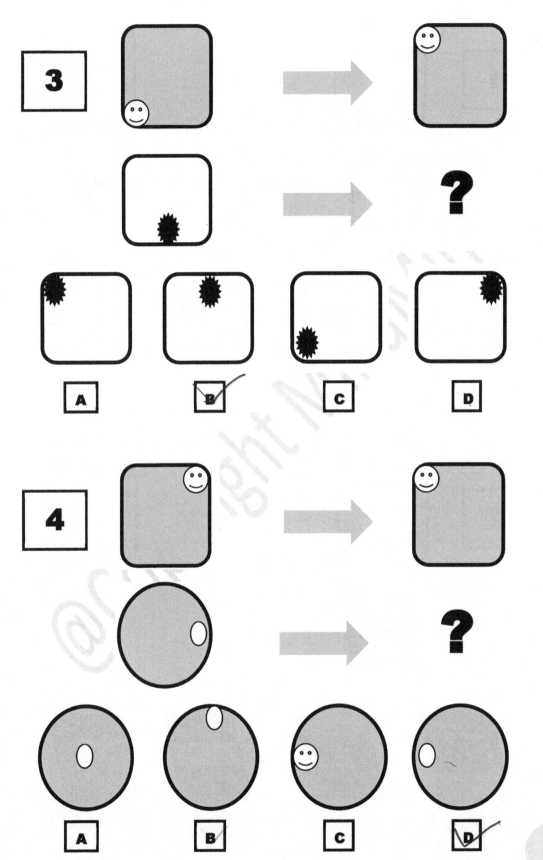

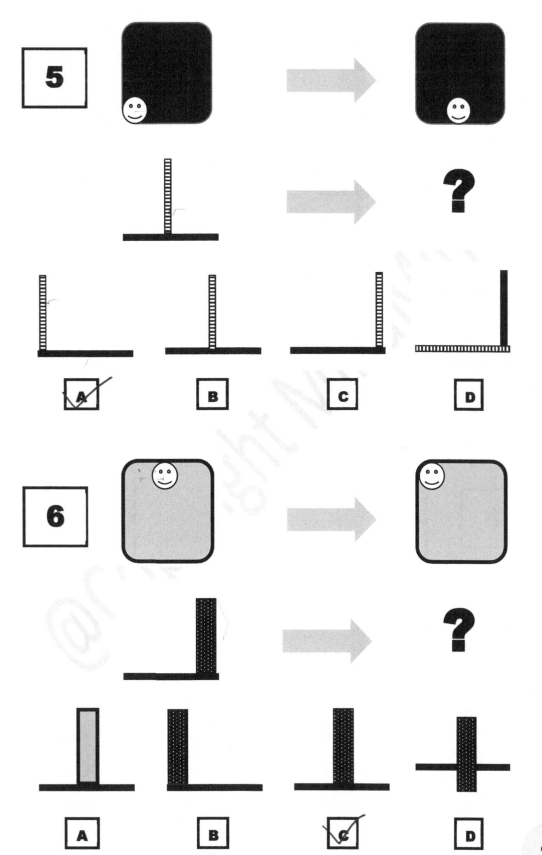

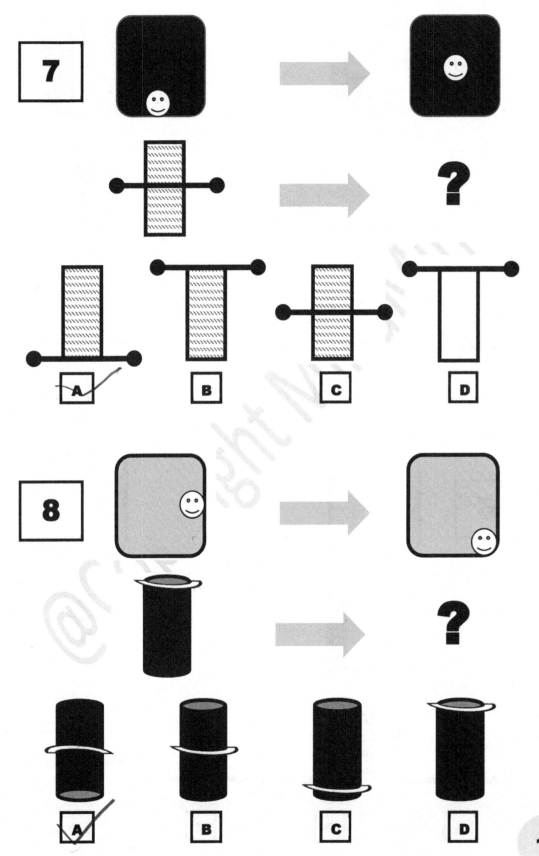

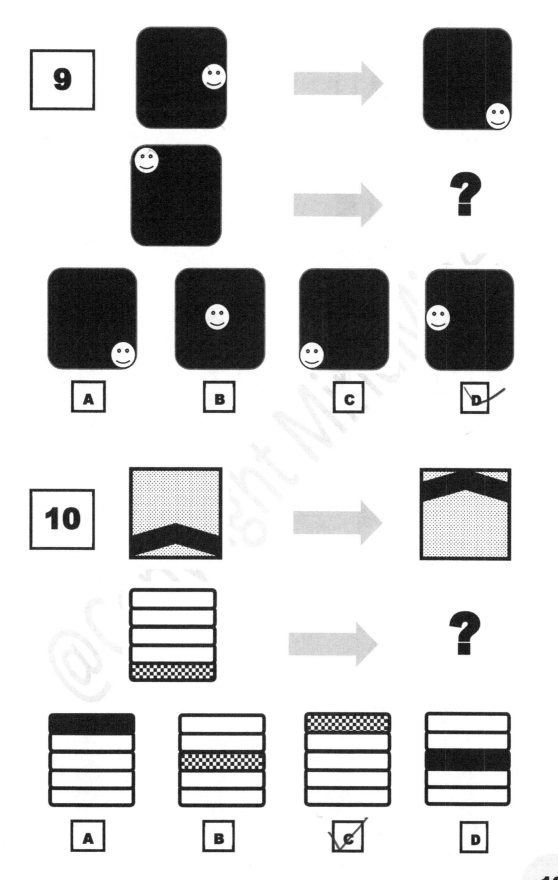

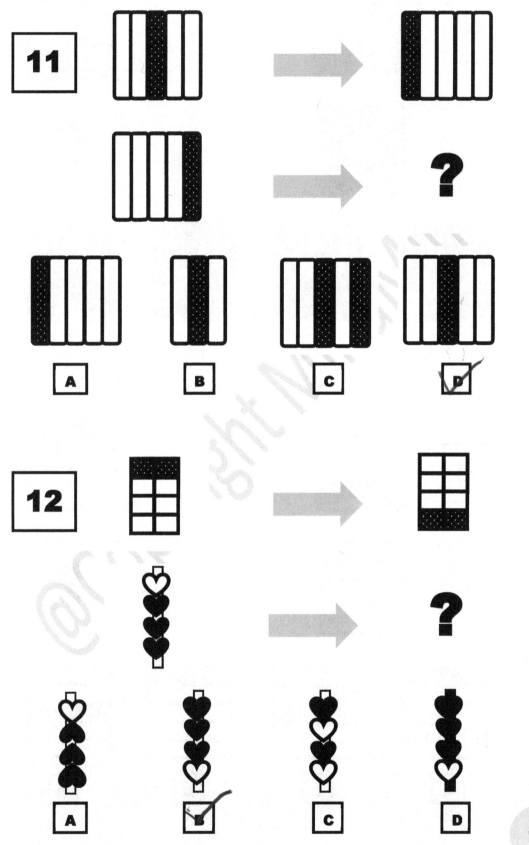

11

A   B   C   D

12

A   B   C   D

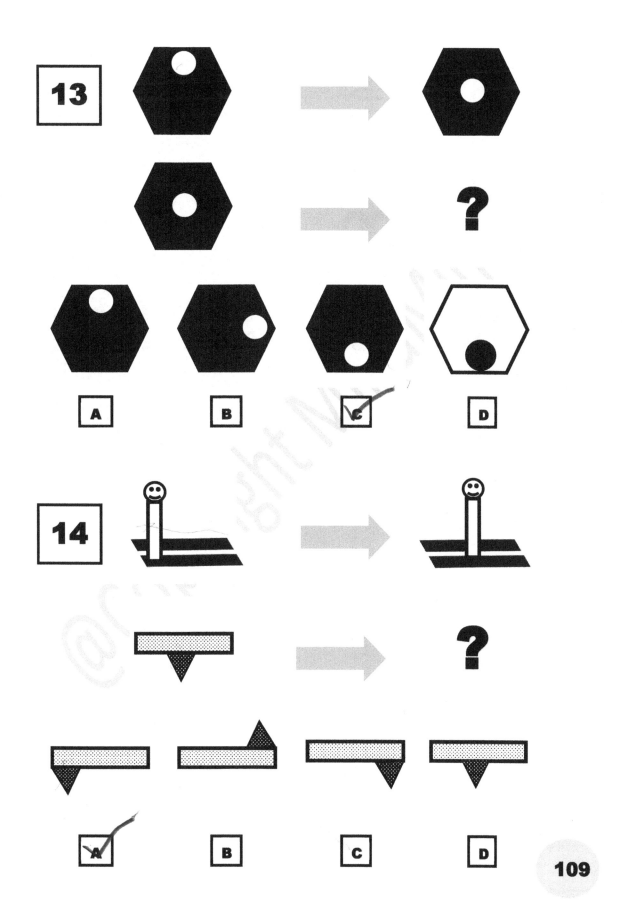

15

A   B   C   D

ANALOGY

SWAP

SWAP POSITION
BRING FRONT/SEND BACK

SWAP POSITION
BRING FRONT/SEND BACK

SWAP POSITION
SWAP PLACE

SWAP
POSITION

SWAP COLOR

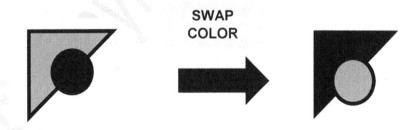

SWAP
COLOR

SWAP COLOR

SWAP
COLOR

SWAP POSITION
SWAP PLACE & SWAP COLOR

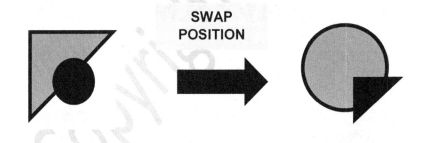

SWAP
POSITION

114

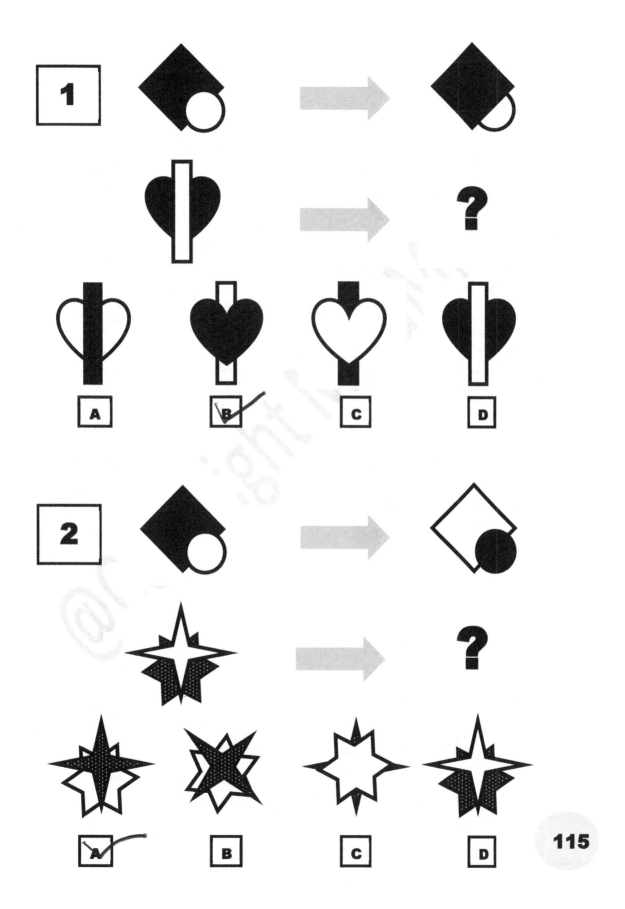

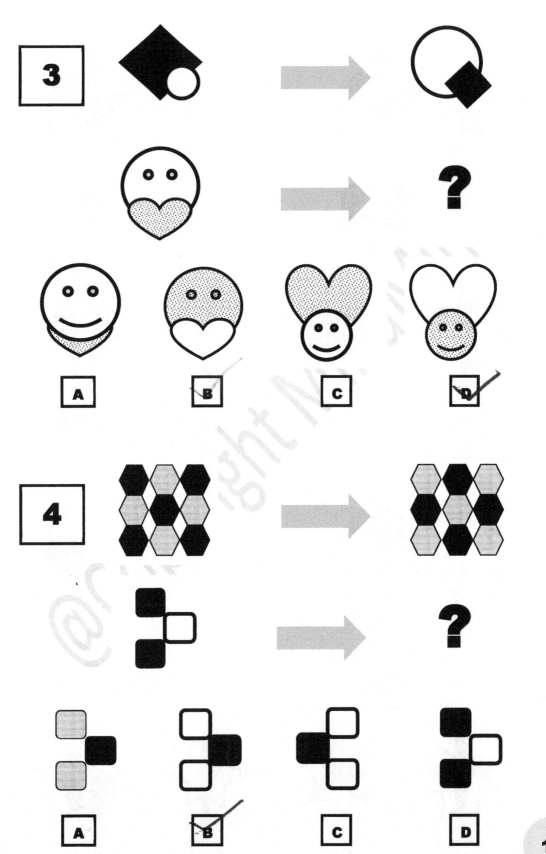

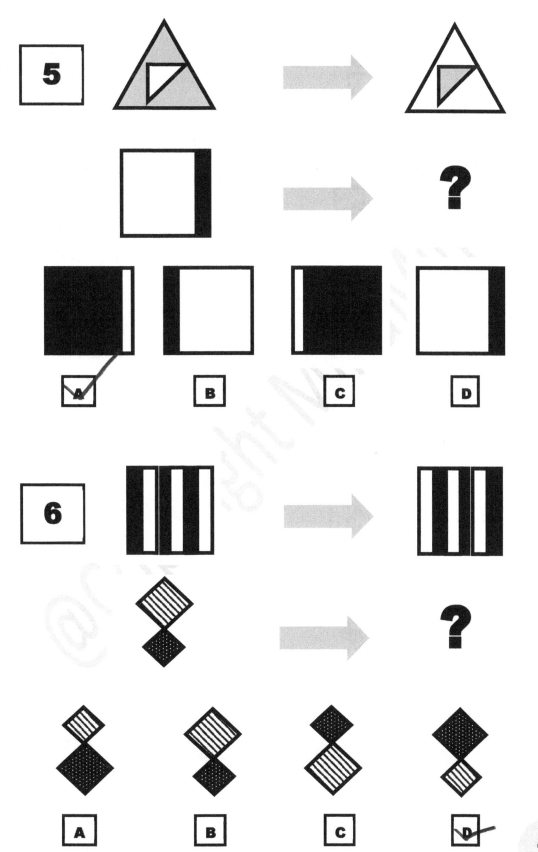

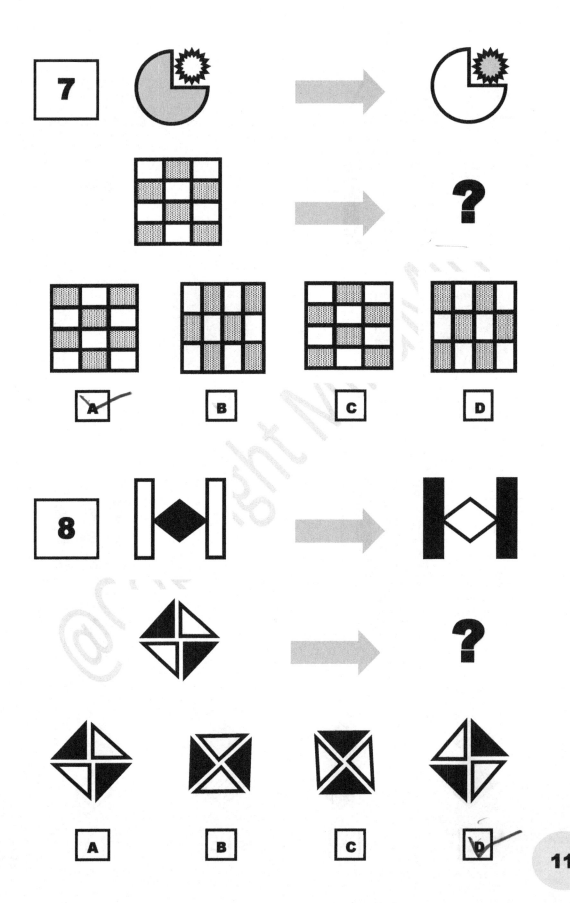

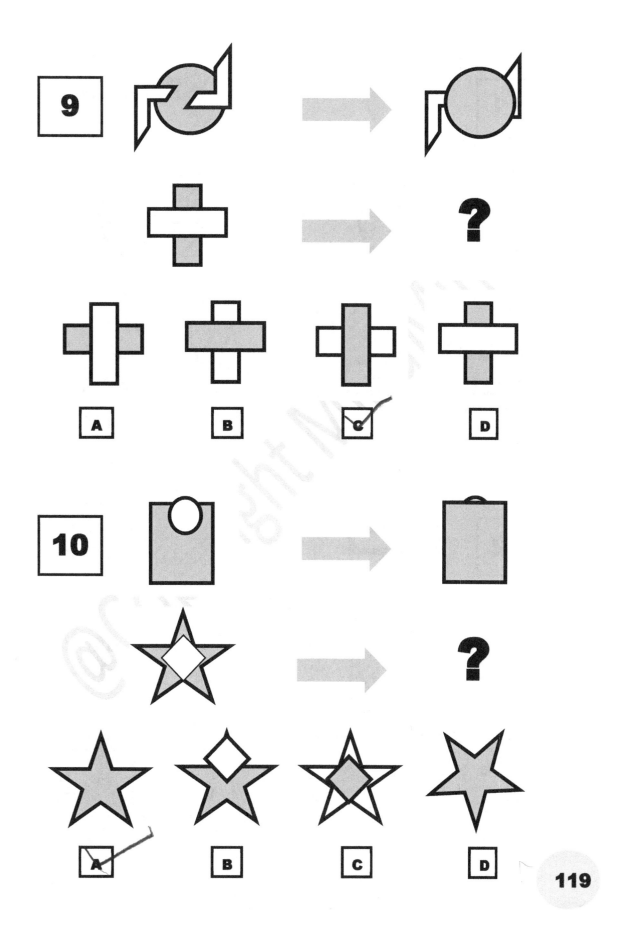

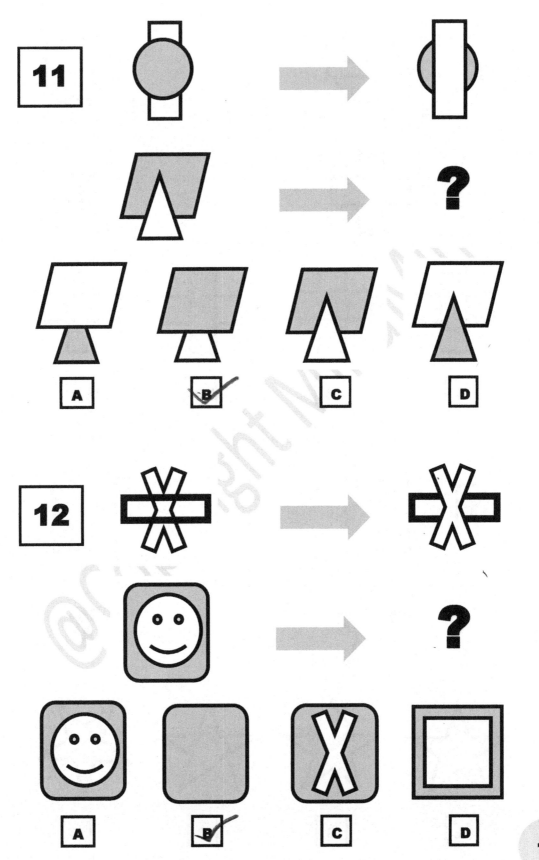

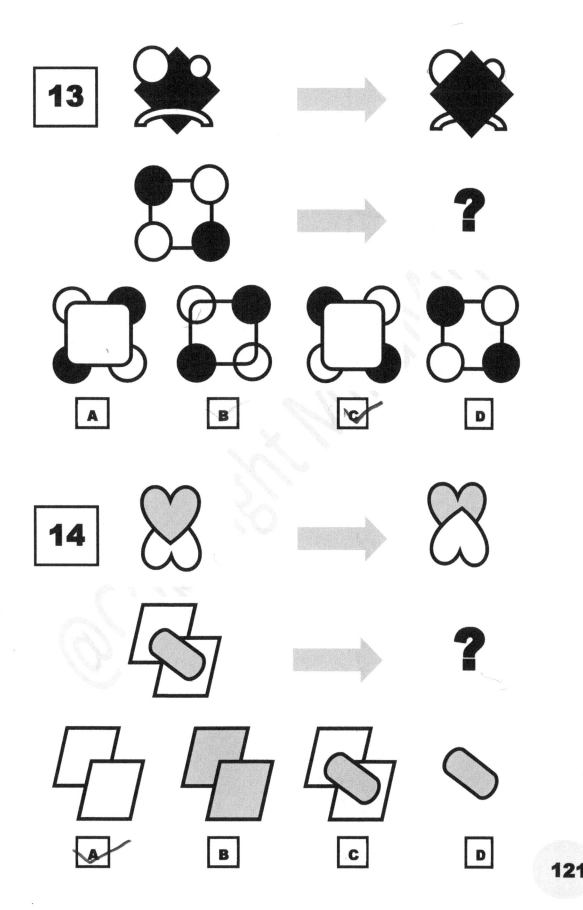

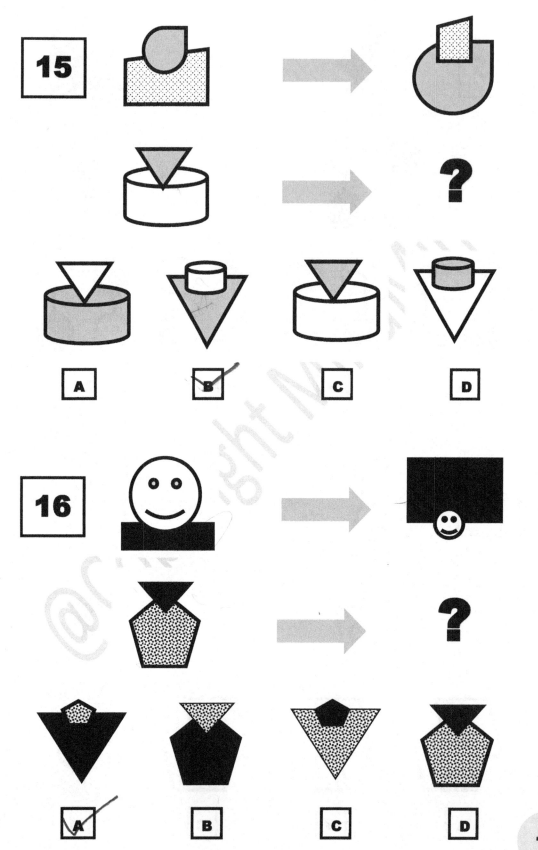

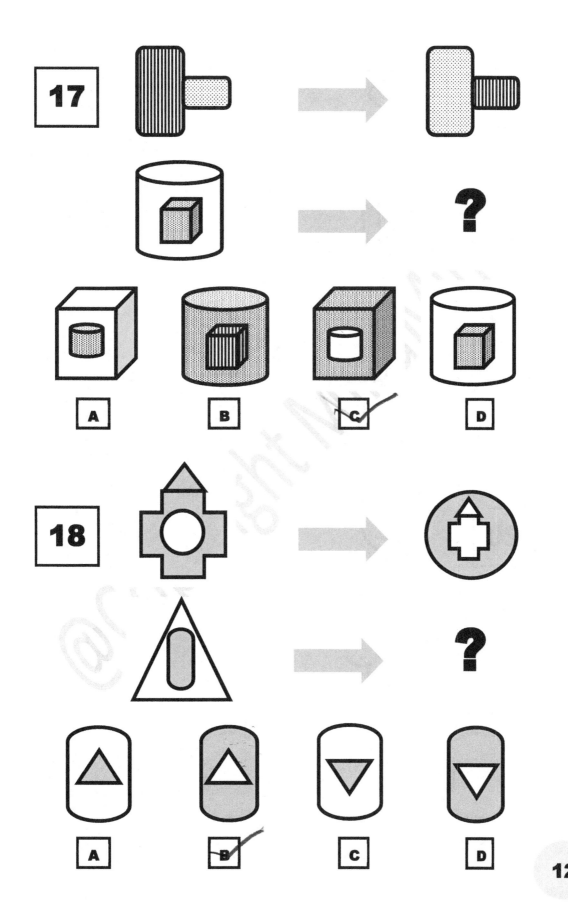

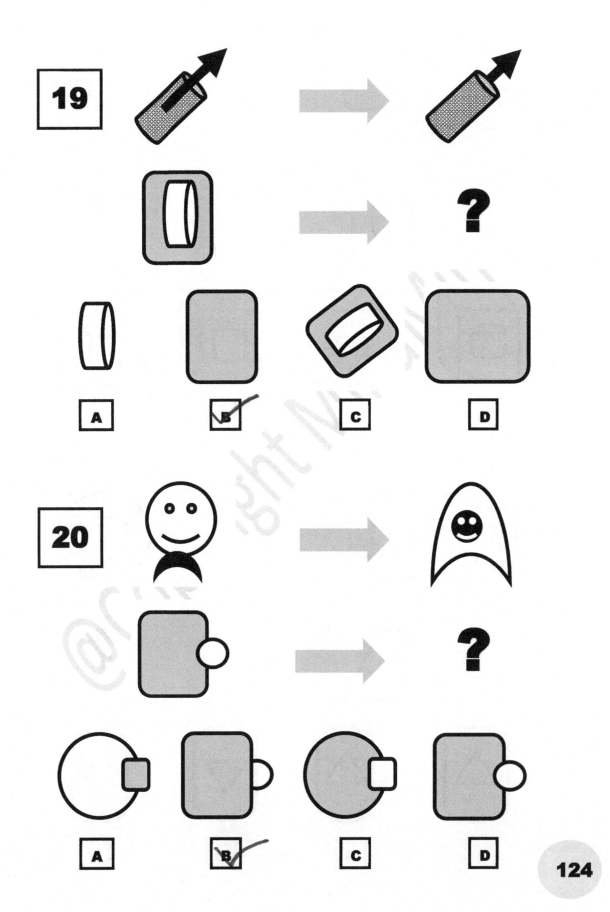

TURN
(ROTATE)

TURN CLOCKWISE

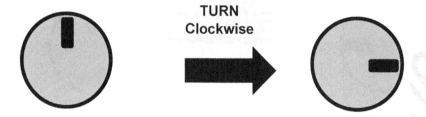

TURN
Clockwise

TURN CLOCKWISE

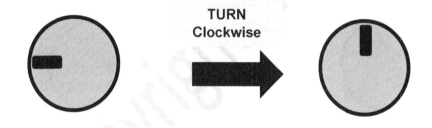

TURN
Clockwise

TURN CLOCKWISE

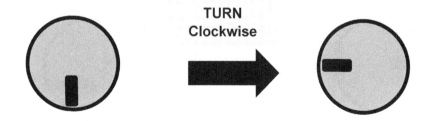

TURN
Clockwise

TURN COUNTER-CLOCKWISE

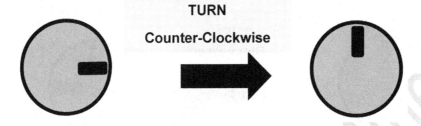

TURN COUNTER-CLOCKWISE

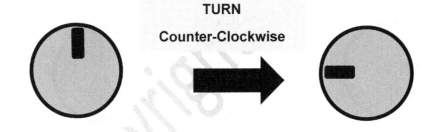

TURN COUNTER-CLOCKWISE

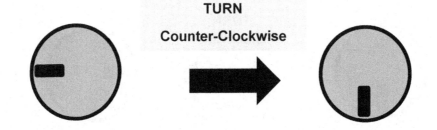

TURN CLOCKWISE

TURN

Clockwise

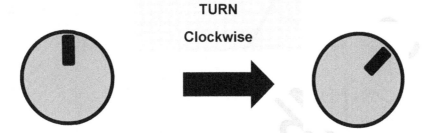

TURN COUNTER-CLOCKWISE

TURN

Counter-Clockwise

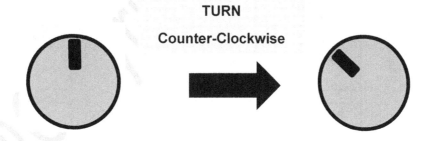

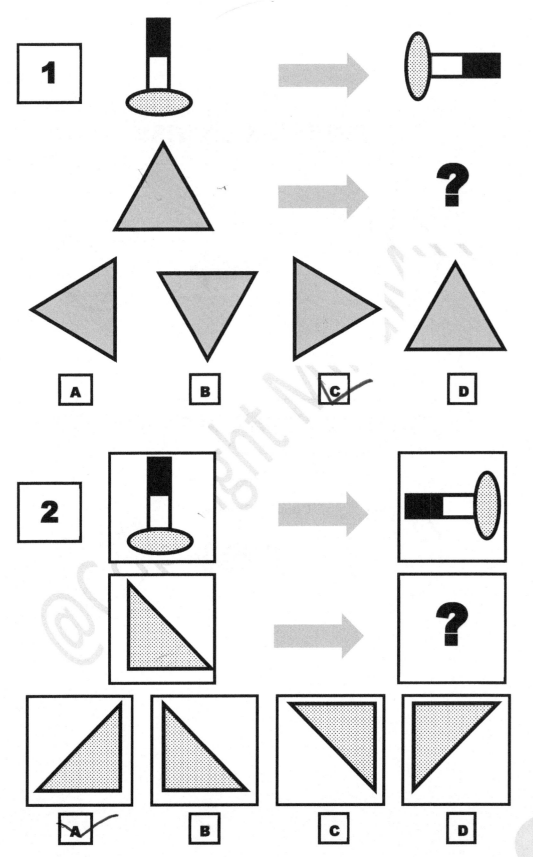

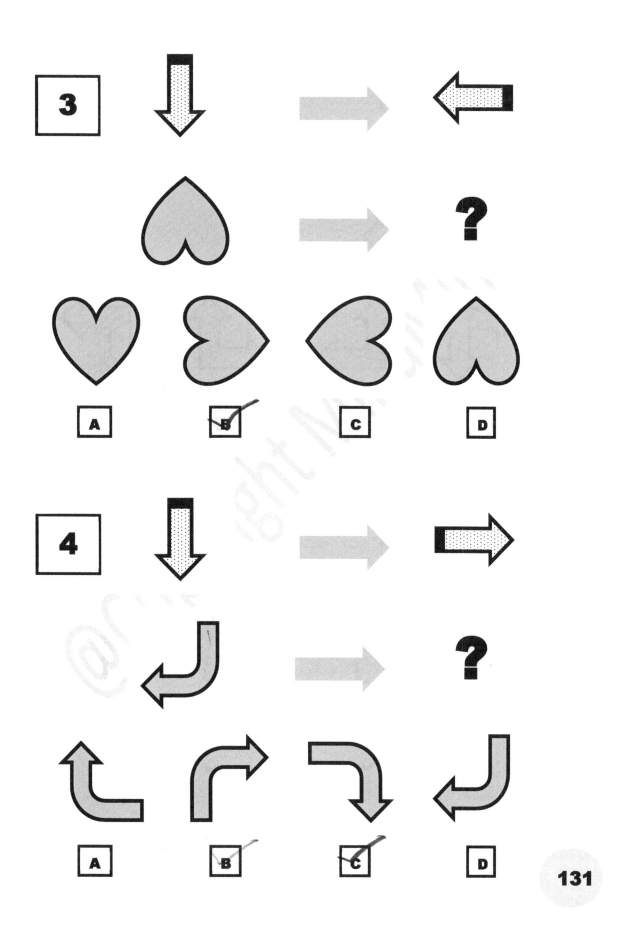

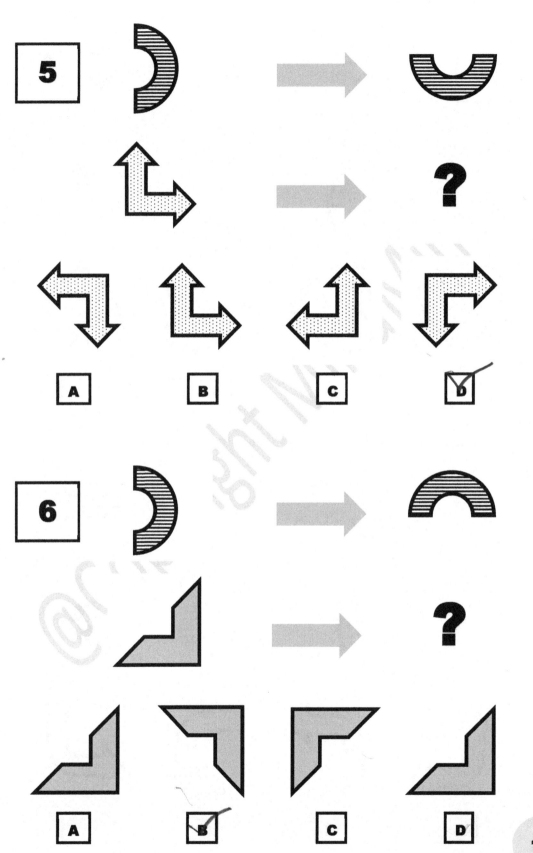

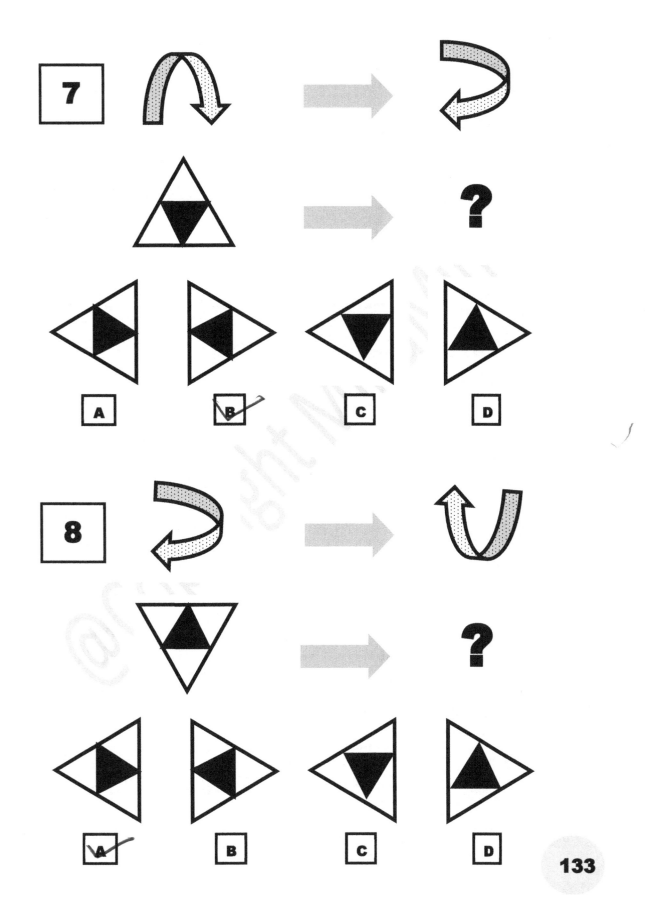

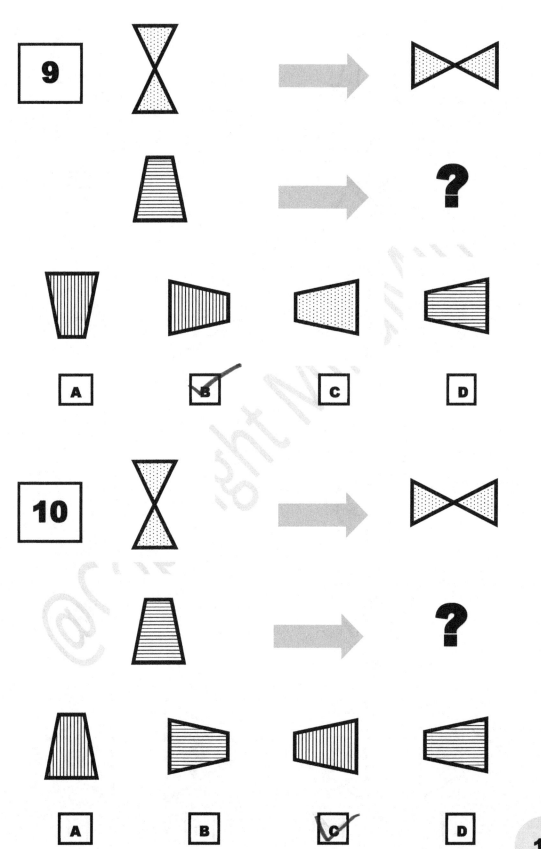

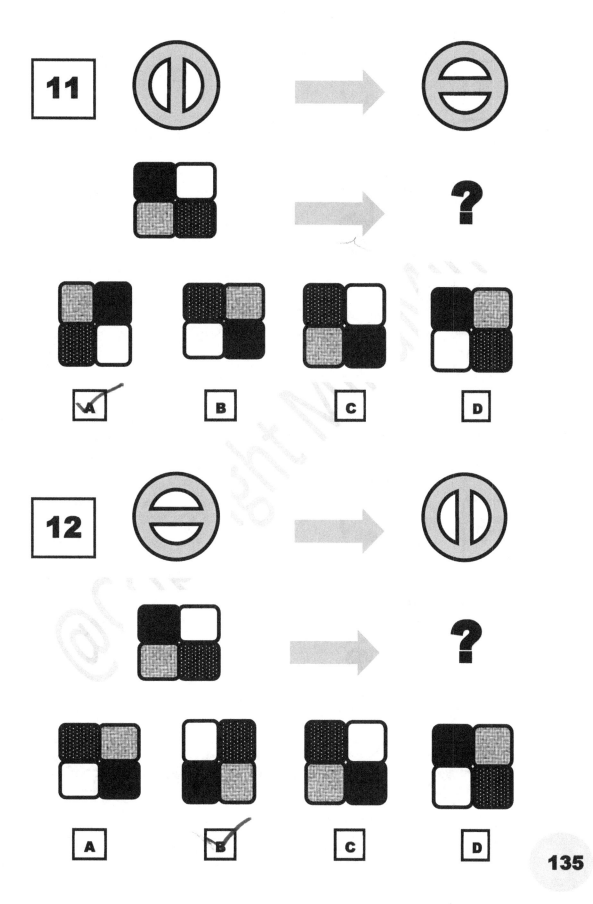

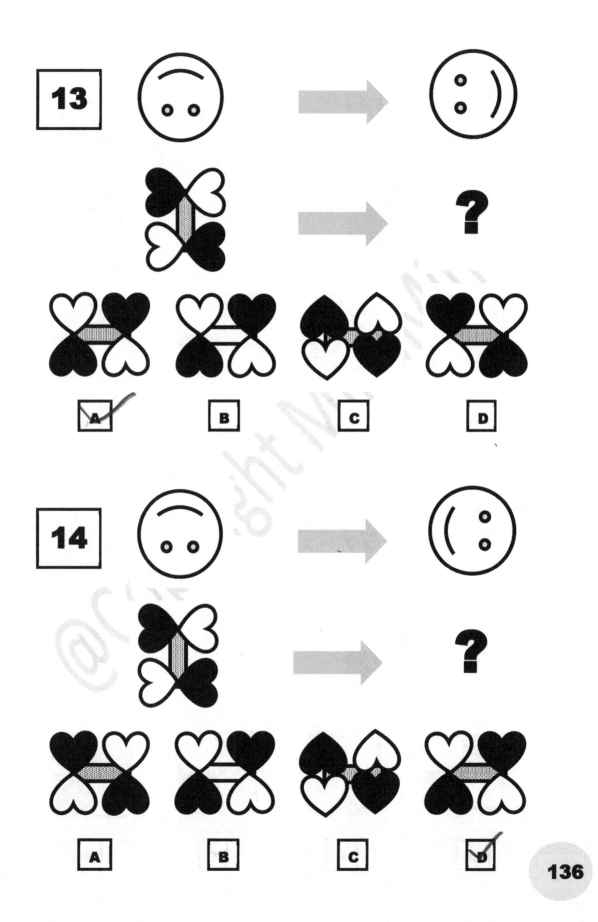

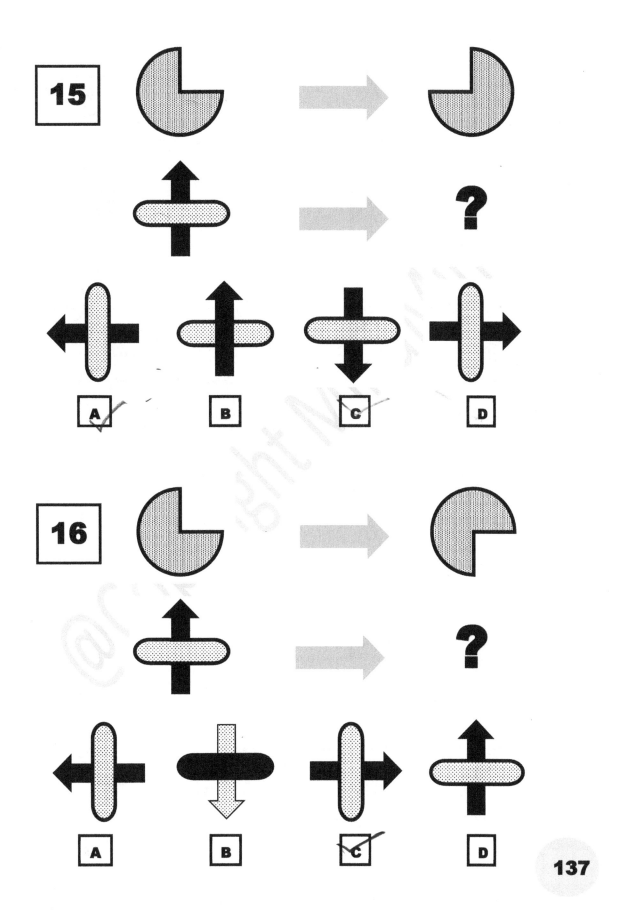

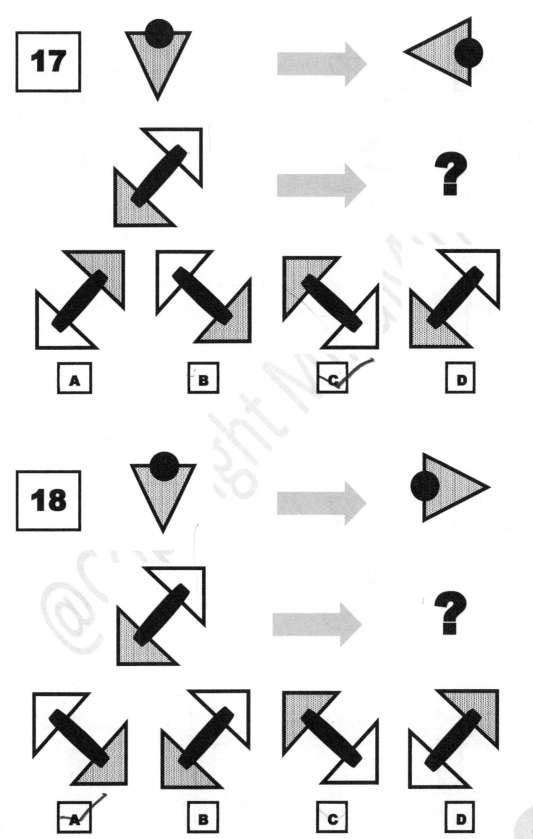

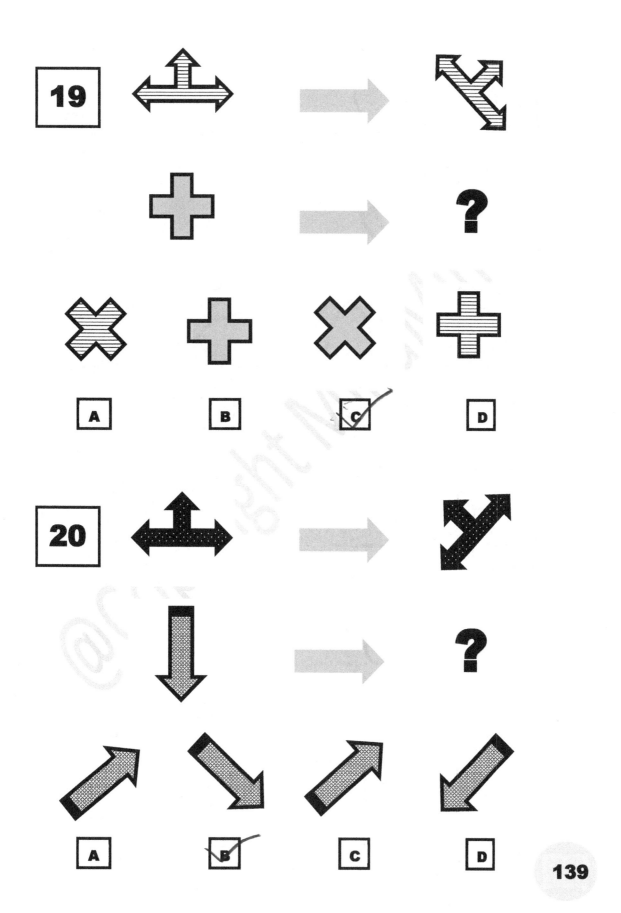

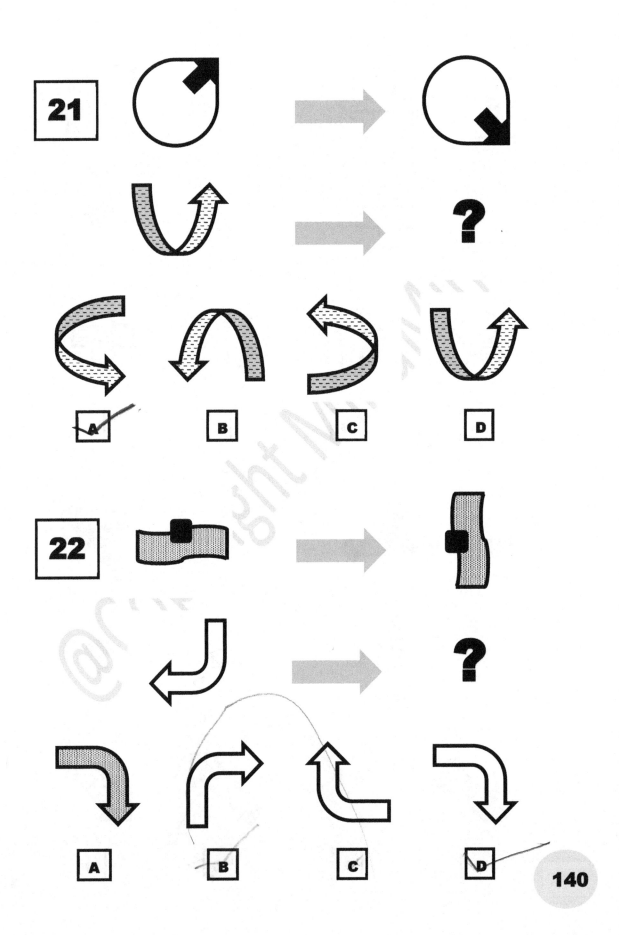

21

A B C D

22

A B C D

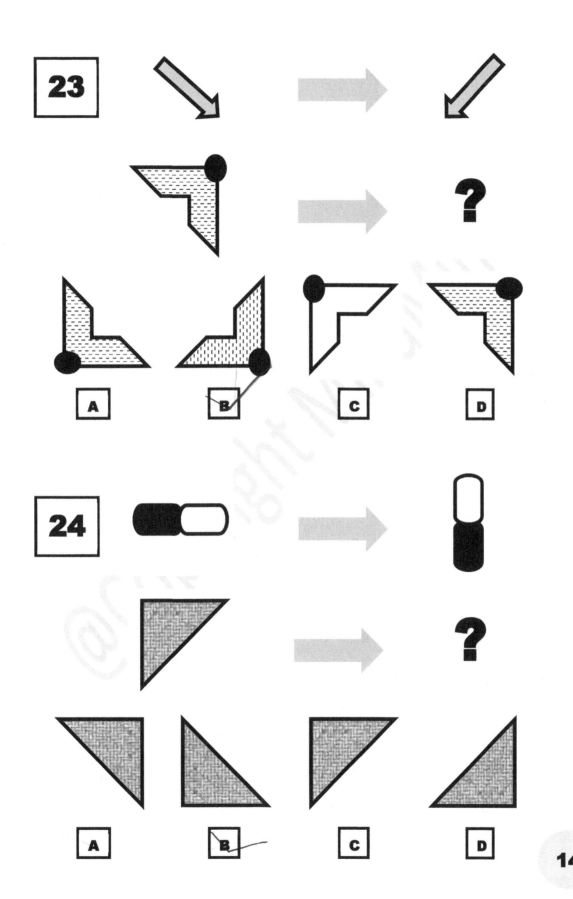

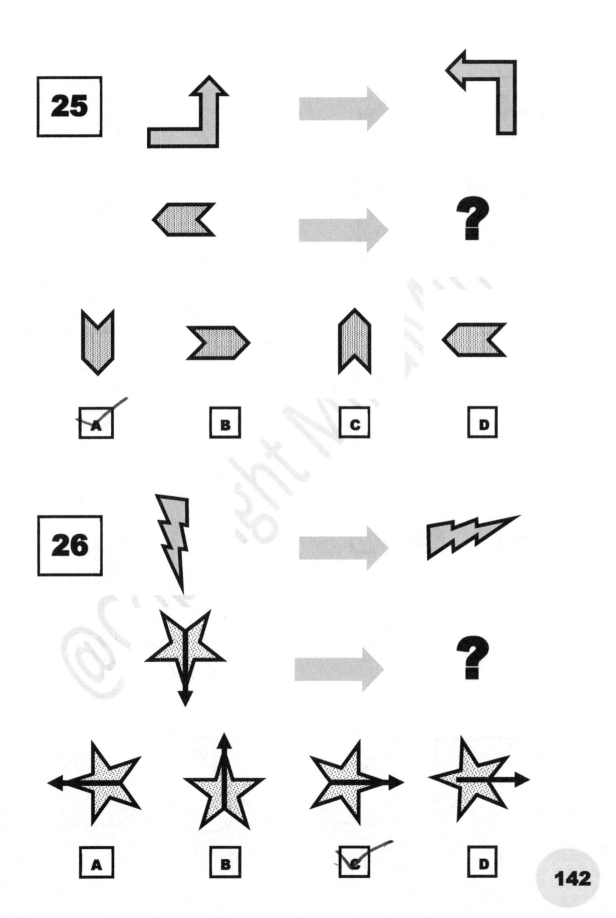

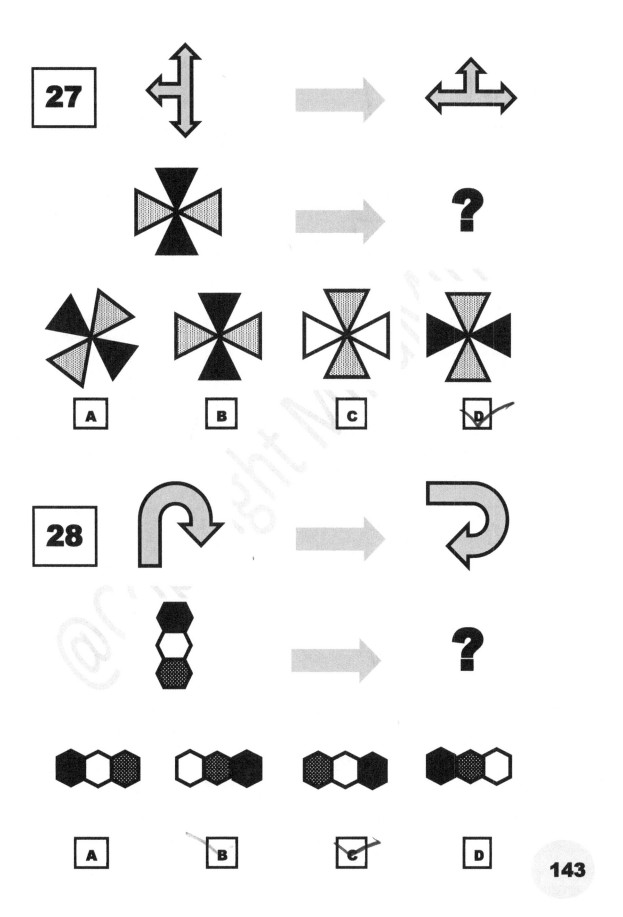

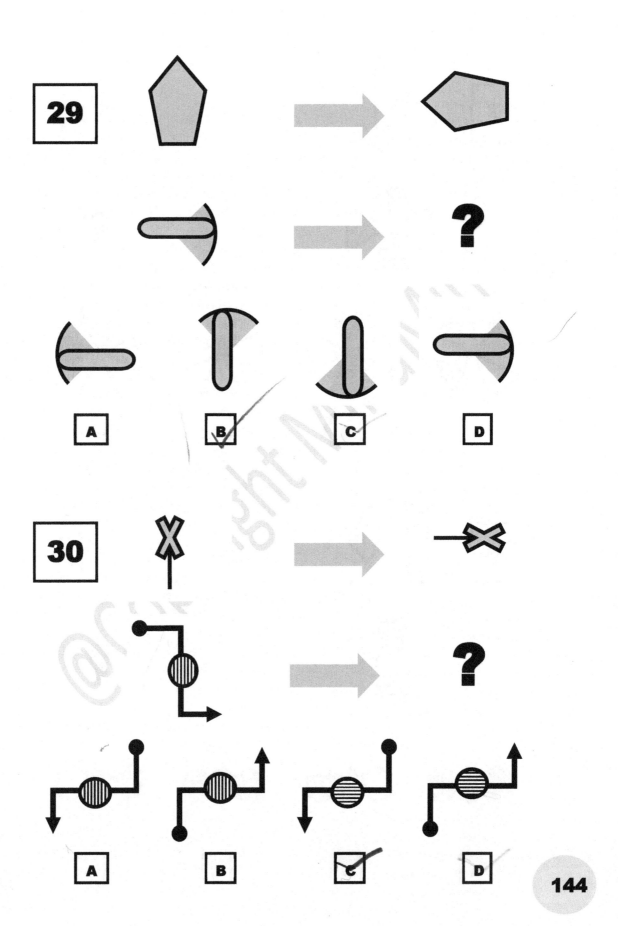

Change #of Sides | Size | Color

FLIP | TURN

MOVE | SWAP | CUT

APPLICATION of ANALOGIES

FULL LENGTH
PRACTICE TEST - 1

Change Color: Fill | Pattern | Outline

Add a Figure | Remove a Figure

Position: Top | Bottom | Left | Right | Corners

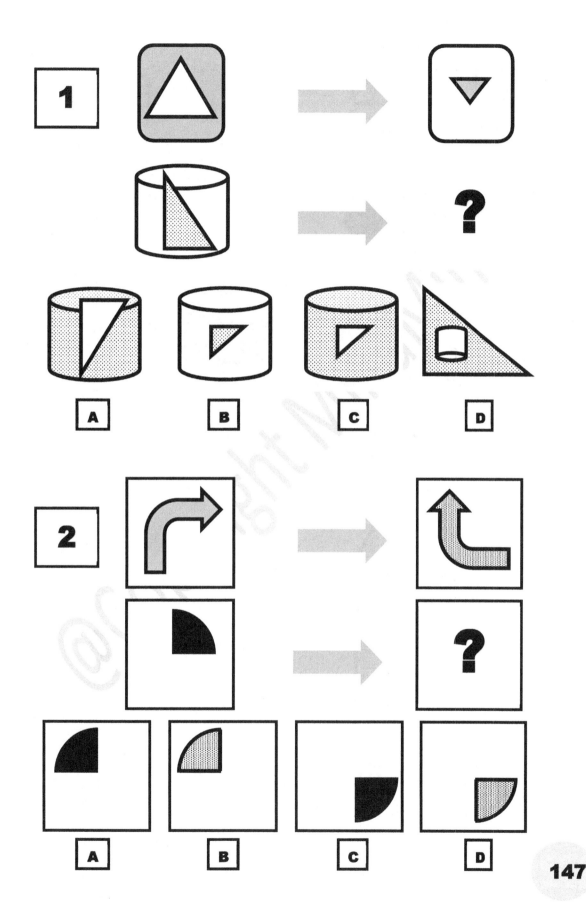

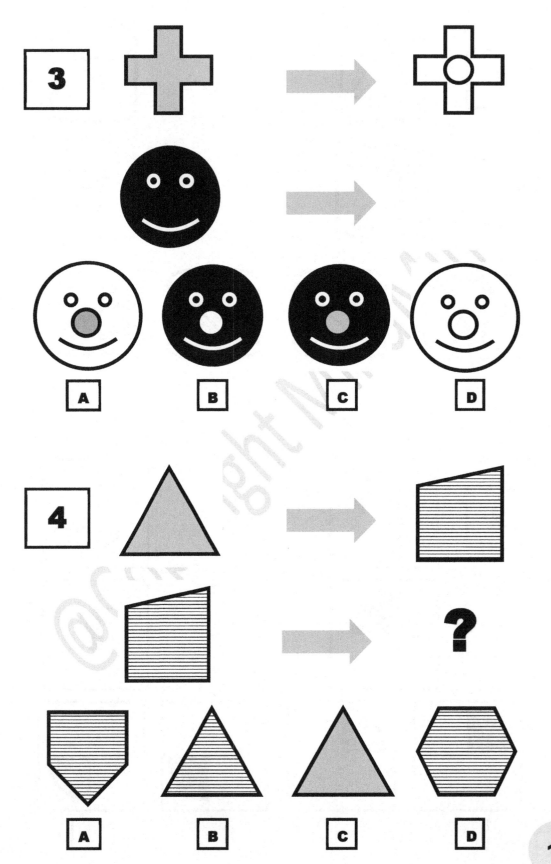

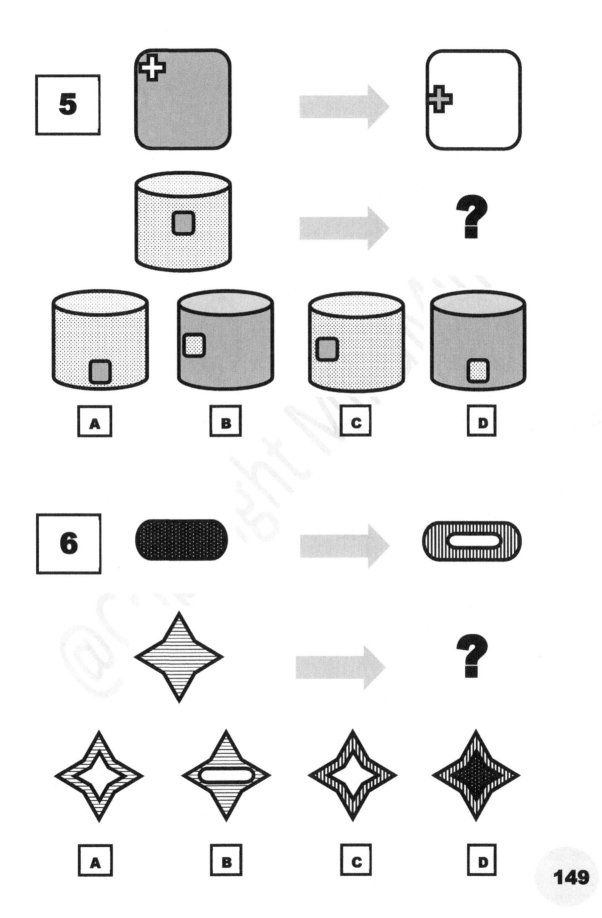

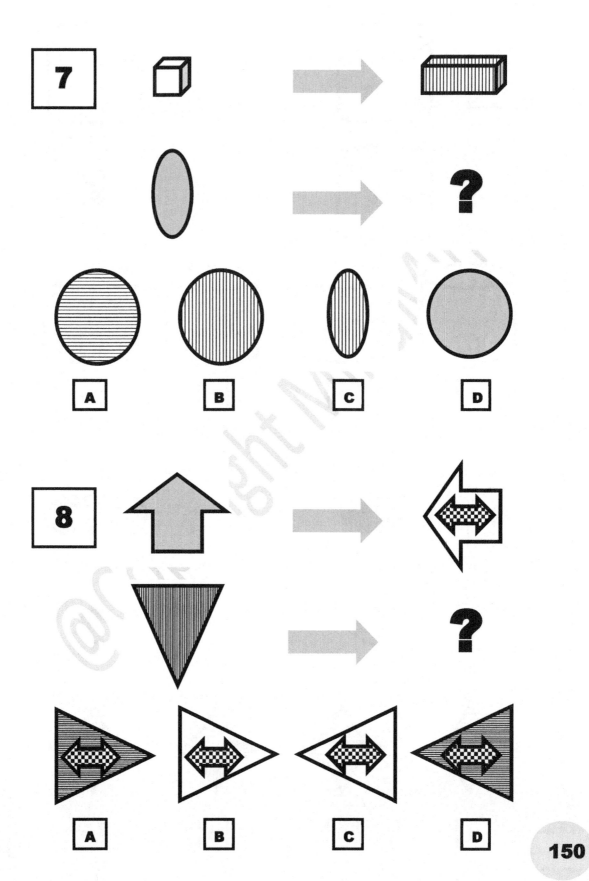

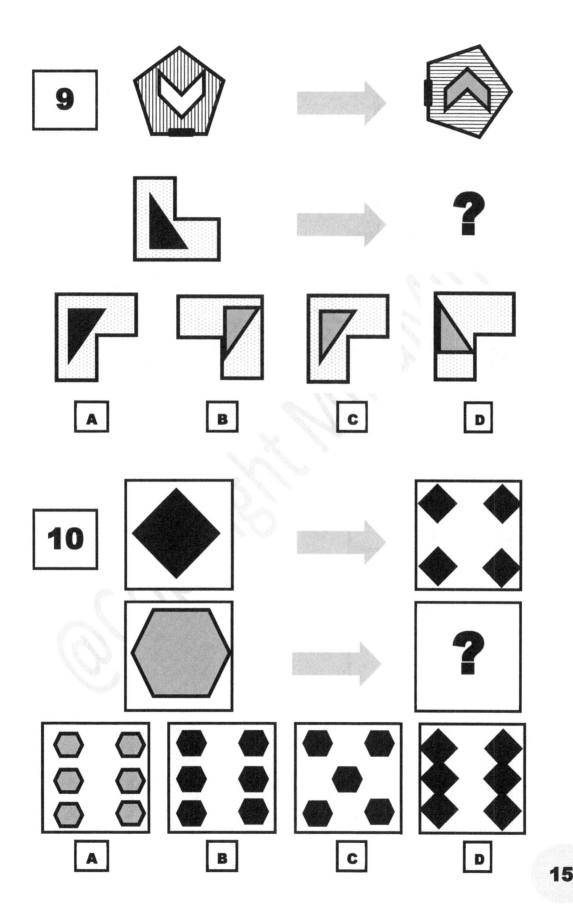

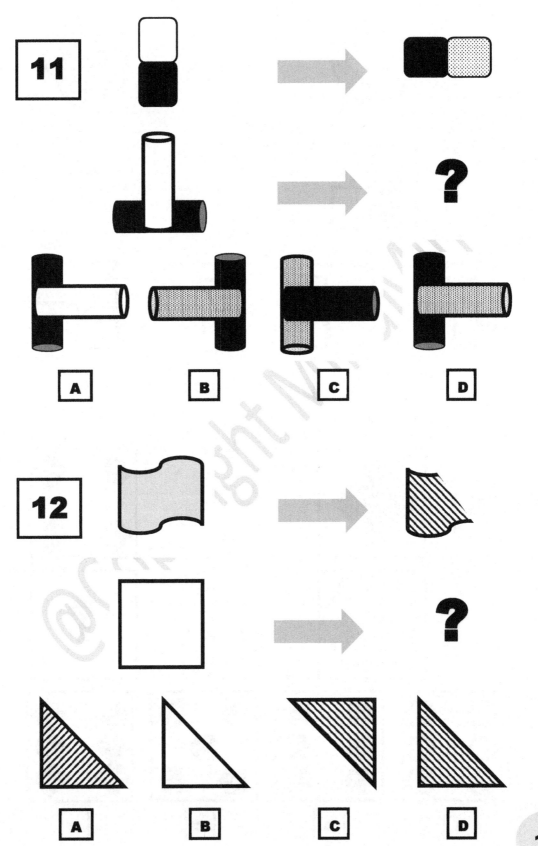

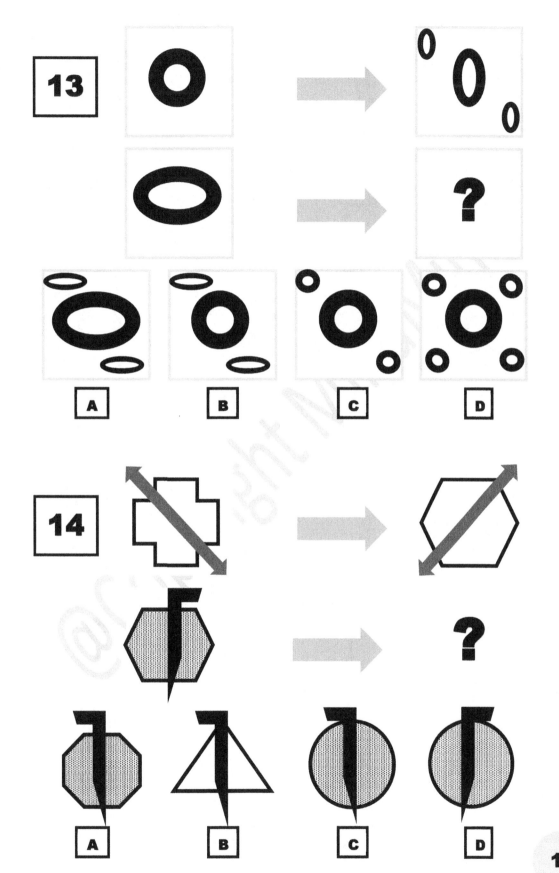

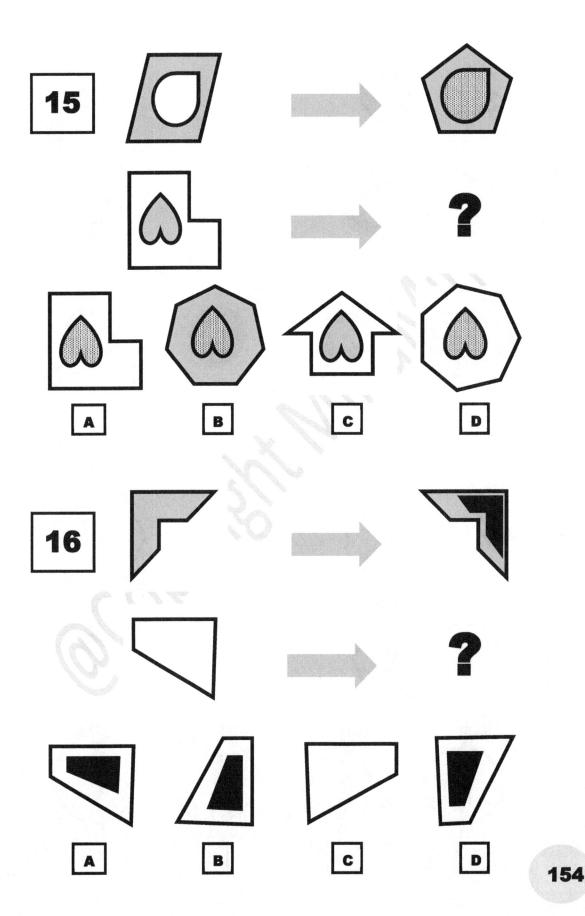

15

A B C D

16

A B C D

154

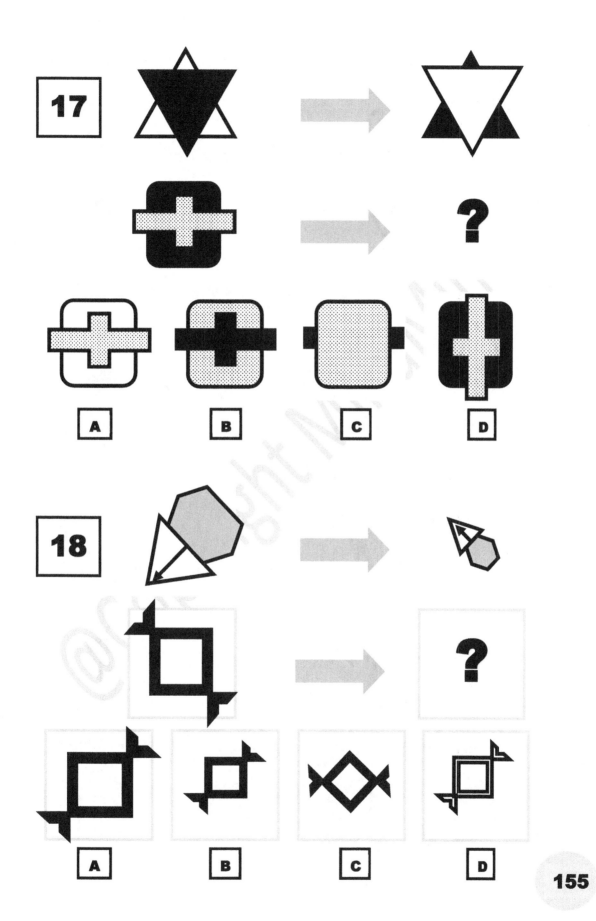

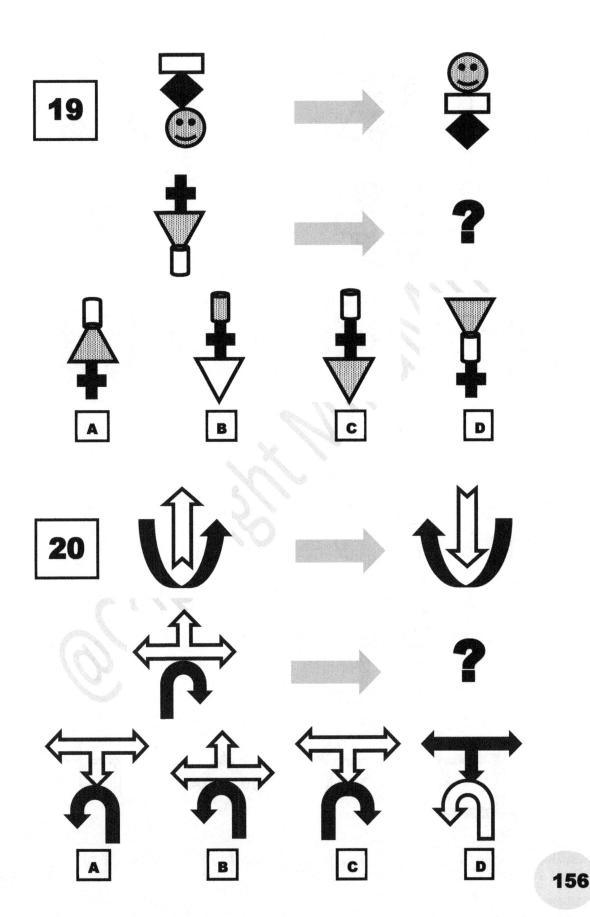

157

APPLICATION of ANALOGIES

FULL LENGTH

PRACTICE TEST - 2

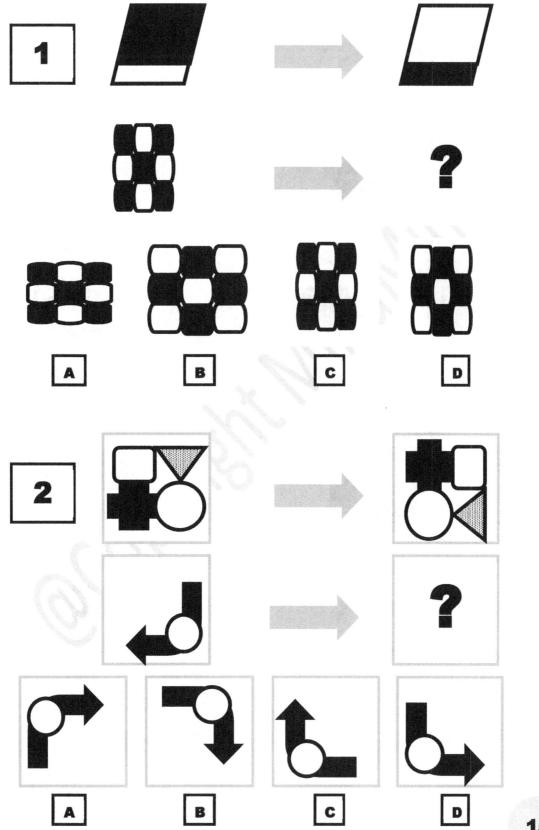

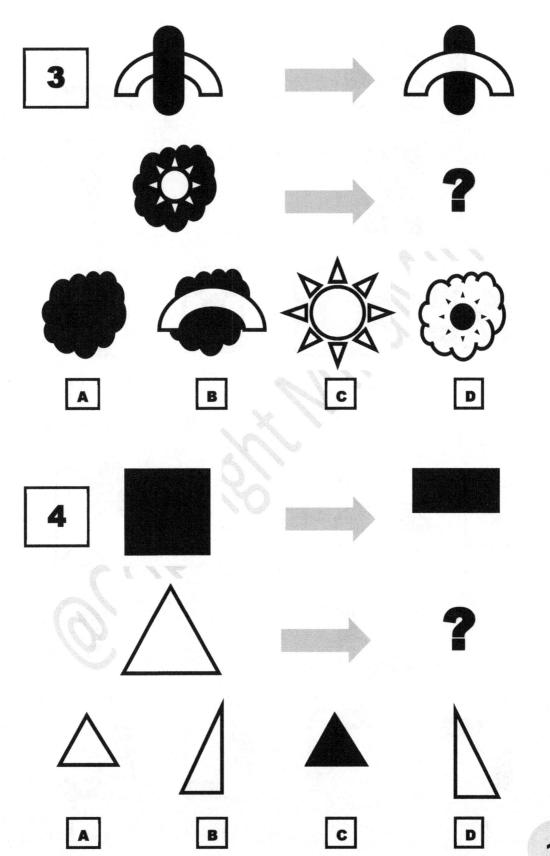

3

A   B   C   D

4

A   B   C   D

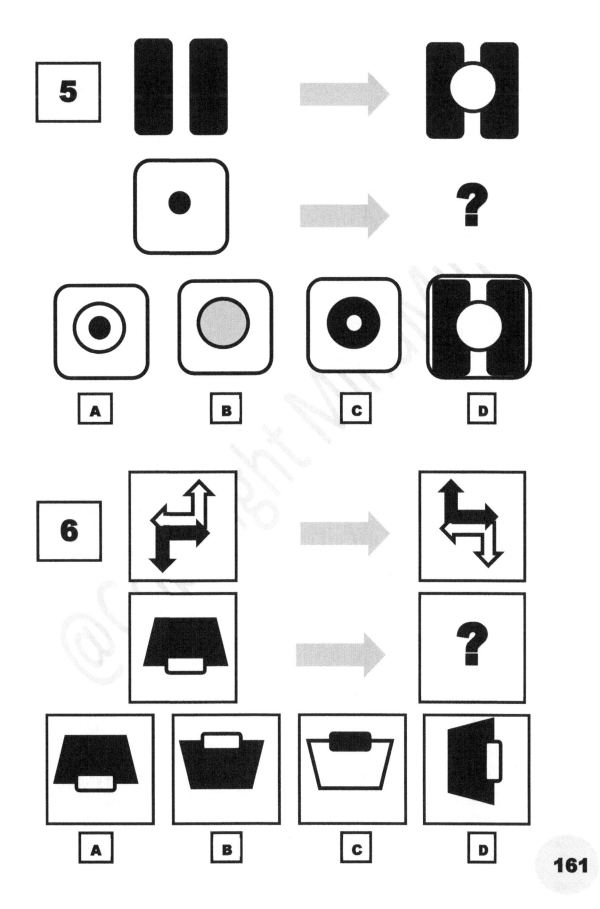

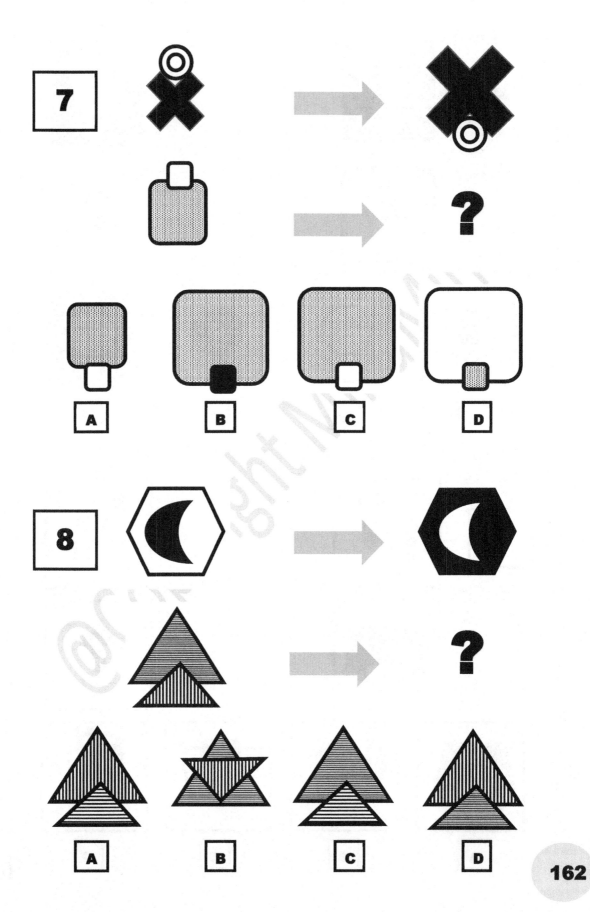

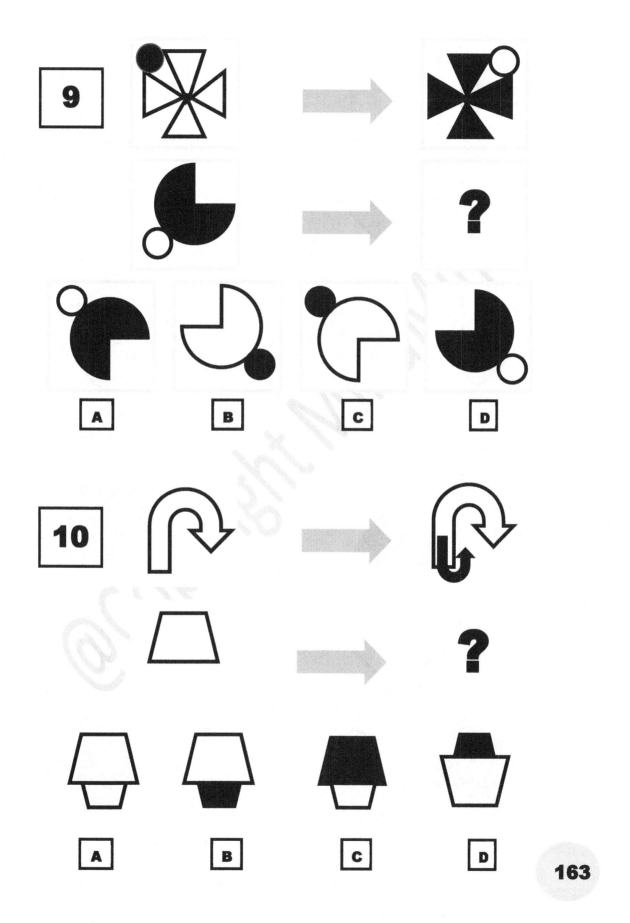

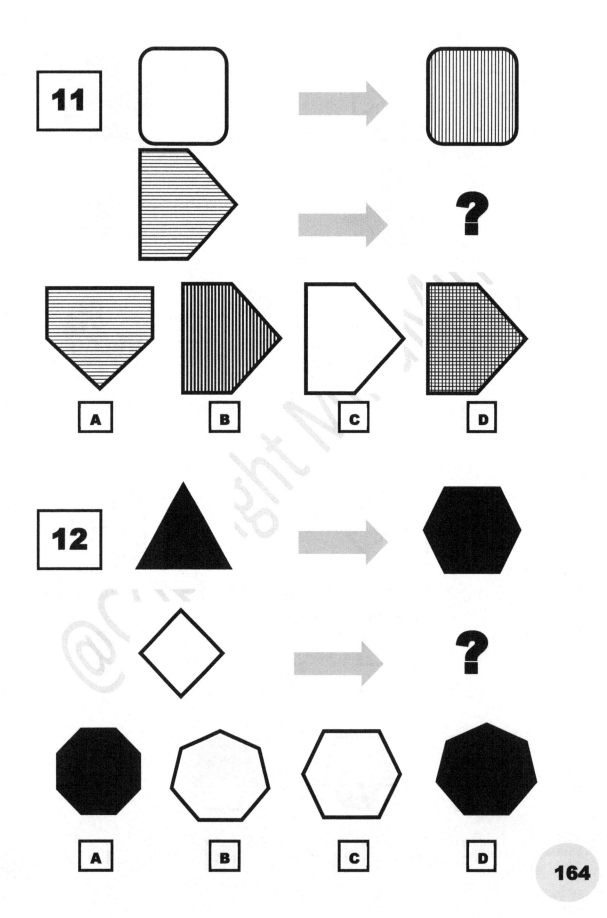

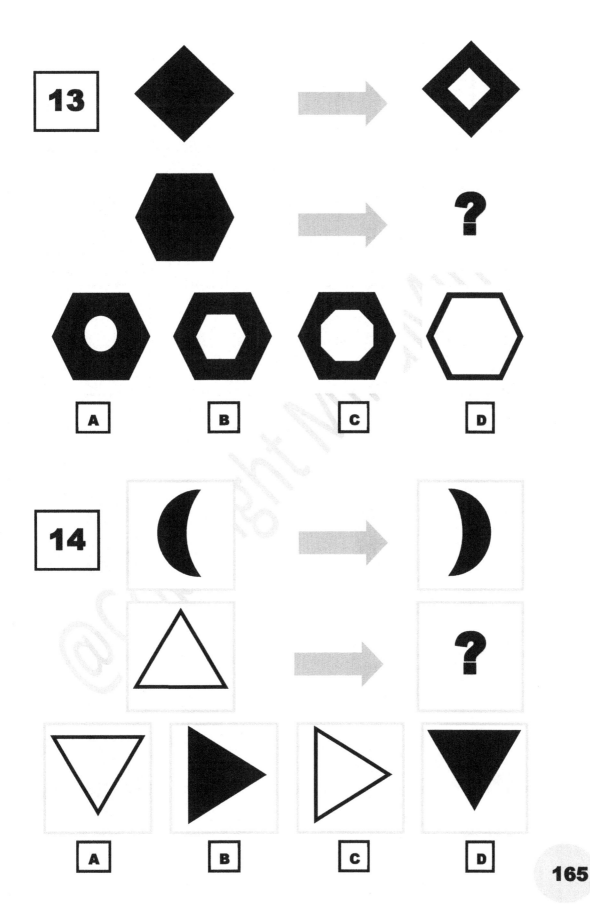

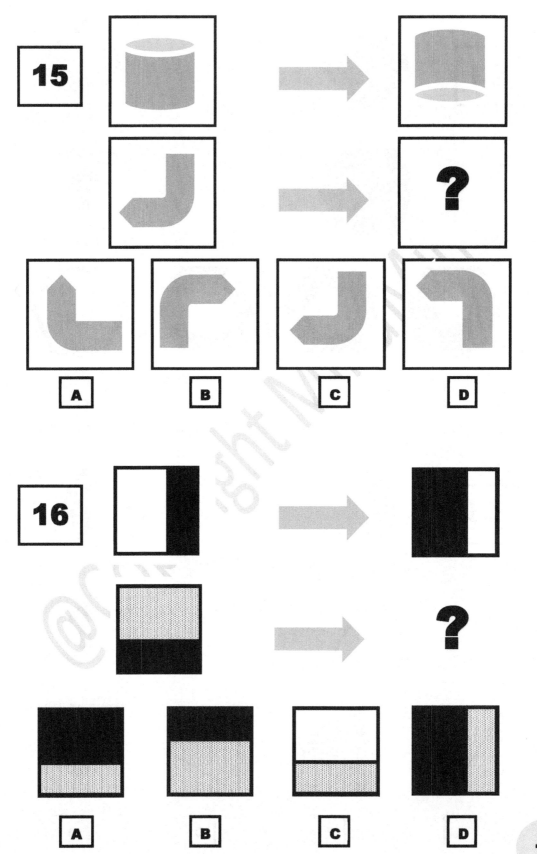

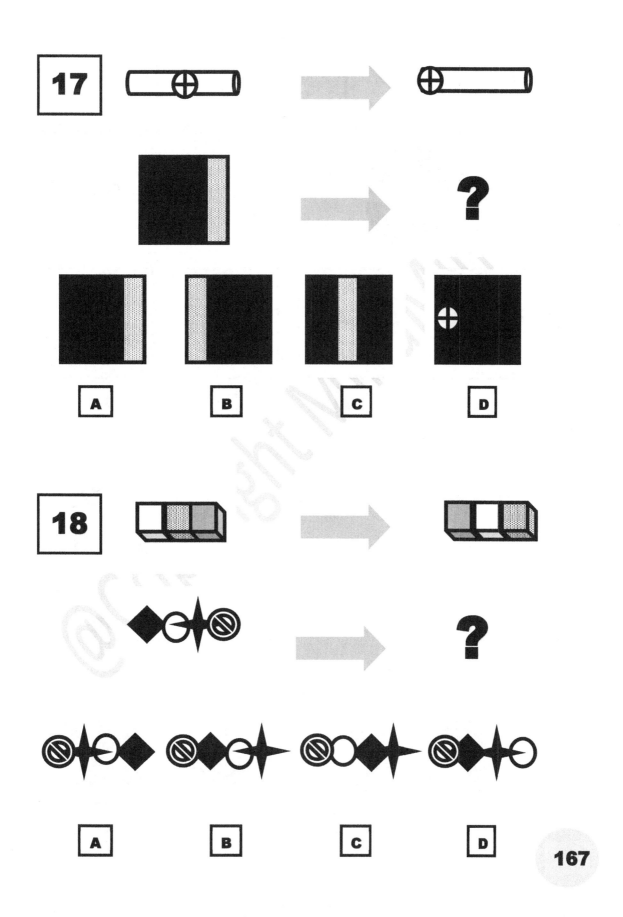

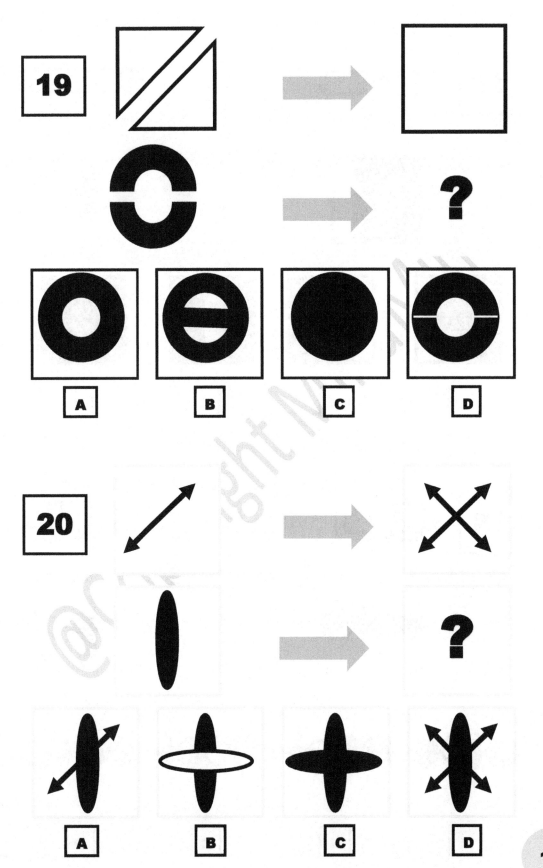

19

20

ANSWERS

CHANGE NUMBER OF SIDES

QUESTION #	ANSWER	ANALOGY
1	D	ADD 1 SIDE MORE (4+1 = 5)
2	C	ADD 2 SIDES MORE (4+2 = 6)
3	D	ADD 3 SIDES MORE (5+3 = 8)
4	B	ADD 4 SIDES MORE (0+4 = 4)
5	A	ADD 5 SIDES MORE (7+5 = 12)
6	C	ADD 6 SIDES MORE (4+6 = 10)
7	A	ADD 7 SIDES MORE (5+7 = 12)
8	C	SUBTRACT 1 SIDE (5-1 = 4)
9	A	SUBTRACT 2 SIDES (8-2 = 6)
10	D	SUBTRACT 2 SIDES (3-3 = 0)
11	C	SUBTRACT 4 SIDES (4-4 = 0)
12	C	SUBTRACT 4 SIDES (10-6 = 4)
13	D	DOUBLE # OF SIDES (4x2=8)
14	D	DOUBLE # OF SIDES (5x2=10)
15	D	TRIPLE # OF SIDES (4x3=12)
16	C	HALF # OF SIDES (6/2=3)
17	C	HALF # OF SIDES (6/2=3)
18	B	SUBTRACT 8 SIDES (8-8 = 0)
19	C	DOUBLE # OF SIDES (4x2=8)
20	D	ADD 3 SIDES MORE (4+3 = 7)
21	B	DOUBLE # OF SIDES (6x2=12)
22	A	ADD 4 SIDES MORE (6+4 = 10)
23	B	HALF # OF SIDES (6/2=3)
24	A	SUBTRACT 6 SIDES (6-6 = 0)
25	A	HALF # OF SIDES (10/2=5)

CHANGE COLOR

QUESTION #	ANSWER	ANALOGY
1	D	CHANGE COLOR(FILL) TO WHITE
2	A	CHANGE COLOR(FILL) TO GRAY ** Solve Left to Right**
3	B	CHANGE COLOR(PATTERN) TO HORIZONTAL LINES
4	C	CHANGE COLOR(PATTERN) TO DIAGONAL LINES ** A – is not the correct pattern **
5	B	CHANGE COLOR(OUTLINE) TO DOTTED LINES
6	A	CHANGE COLOR(OUTLINE) TO SOLID LINE
7	C	CHANGE COLOR(FILL) TO WHITE ** Solve Left to Right**
8	A	CHANGE COLOR(FILL) TO WHITE ** Solve Left to Right**
9	C	CHANGE COLOR(FILL) TO GRAY ** Solve Left to Right**
10	D	CHANGE COLOR(PATTERN) TO DOTS
11	C	CHANGE COLOR(FILL) OF INSIDE SHAPE TO WHITE

		** Solve Left to Right**
12	A	CHANGE COLOR(FILL) OF OUTSIDE SHAPES <u>TO</u> WHITE ** Solve Left to Right**
13	C	CHANGE COLOR(PATTERN) OF TOP SHAPE <u>TO</u> "CHECKER BOARD" CHANGE COLOR(FILL) OF BOTTOM SHAPE <u>TO</u> WHITE
14	D	CHANGE COLOR(FILL) OF TOP SHAPE <u>TO</u> WHITE CHANGE COLOR(PATTERN) OF BOTTOM SHAPE <u>TO</u> DIAGONAL LINES
15	D	CHANGE COLOR(PATTERN) <u>TO</u> HORIZONTAL LINES

CHANGE SIZE

QUESTION #	ANSWER	ANALOGY
1	B	MAKE BIG (Stretch Width & Height)
2	C	MAKE BIG (Stretch Width & Height)
3	A	MAKE BIG (Stretch Width & Height)
4	A	MAKE BIG (Stretch Width & Height)
5	C	MAKE BIG (Stretch Width & Height)
6	B	MAKE SMALL (Squeeze Width & Height)
7	A	MAKE SMALL (Squeeze Width & Height)
8	D	MAKE SMALL
9	B	MAKE SMALL (Squeeze Width & Height)
10	C	MAKE SMALL
11	C	MAKE BIG (Stretch Horizontally only)

12	A	MAKE BIG (Stretch Vertically only)
13	B	MAKE BIG (Stretch Vertically only)
14	D	MAKE BIG (Stretch Horizontally only)
15	D	MAKE BIG (Stretch Vertically only)
16	A	MAKE BIG (Stretch Horizontally only)
17	C	MAKE SMALL (Squeeze Vertically Only)
18	A	MAKE SMALL (Squeeze Vertically Only)
19	C	MAKE SMALL (Squeeze Vertically Only)
20	A	MAKE SMALL (Squeeze Horizontally Only)
21	D	MAKE SMALL (Squeeze Horizontally Only)
22	A	MAKE SMALL (Squeeze Horizontally Only)

23	**B**	MAKE SMALL (Squeeze Horizontally Only)
24	**B**	MAKE SMALL (Squeeze Horizontally Only)
25	**A**	MAKE SMALL (Squeeze Horizontally Only)

FLIP (REFLECTION)

QUESTION #	ANSWER	ANALOGY
1	C	FLIP UPSIDE DOWN
2	D	FLIP UPSIDE DOWN
3	B	FLIP UPSIDE DOWN
4	B	FLIP UPSIDE DOWN
5	C	FLIP UPSIDE DOWN
6	A	FLIP UPSIDE DOWN
7	C	FLIP UPSIDE DOWN
8	D	FLIP UPSIDE DOWN
9	B	FLIP UPSIDE DOWN
10	C	FLIP UPSIDE DOWN ** if "C" is not given, "A" becomes right answer. Analogy: Generic FLIP
11	D	FLIP SIDEWAYS
12	A	FLIP SIDEWAYS
13	C	FLIP SIDEWAYS
14	A	FLIP SIDEWAYS
15	D	FLIP SIDEWAYS
16	A	FLIP SIDEWAYS
17	B	FLIP SIDEWAYS
18	C	FLIP SIDEWAYS
19	A	FLIP SIDEWAYS
20	B	FLIP SIDEWAYS

CUT

QUESTION #	ANSWER	ANALOGY
1	B	CUT BOTTOM
2	C	CUT TOP
3	D	CUT RIGHT
4	B	CUT LEFT
5	C	CUT BOTTOM
6	D	CUT TOP
7	C	CUT TOP DIAGONALLY
8	A	CUT RIGHT
9	B	CUT BOTTOM
10	B	CUT TOP

ADD/REMOVE

QUESTION #	ANSWER	ANALOGY
1	C	ADD A WHITE TRAINGLE INSIDE
2	A	ADD A WHITE CYLINDER INSIDE
3	D	ADD A WHITE SMILEY AT BOTTOM-MIDDLE
4	A	ADD A WHITE OCTAGON IN THE MIDDLE
5	B	ADD A DOTTED, POINTING UP TRAINAGLE INSIDE
6	A	ADD A BLACK VERTICAL STRIP
7	D	ADD A BLCK BOX OUTSIDE
8	A	ADD A SMALLER SAME SHAPE WITH WHITE COLOR INSIDE
9	A	ADD A SMALLER SAME SHAPE WITH WHITE COLOR INSIDE
10	C	ADD A SMALLER SAME SHAPE (DONUT) WITH WHITE COLOR INSIDE
11	D	ADD A WHITE HORIZONTAL STRIP

12	C	ADD A BLACK DONUT IN THE MIDDLE
13	A	ADD SAME SHAPE WITH WHITE COLOR ON THE RIGHT
14	A	REMOVE A SIDE
15	A	REMOVE INSIDE SHAPE
16	B	REMOVE WHITE TRIANGLE (REMOVE ONE SHAPE)
17	C	REMOVE BLACK COLOR SHAPE
18	B	REMOVE INSIDE SHAPE
19	C	REMOVE BOTTOM SHAPE
20	D	REMOVE MIDDLE SHAPE

MOVE

QUESTION #	ANSWER	ANALOGY
1	C	MOVE RIGHT ALL THE WAY
2	A	MOVE DOWN ALL THE WAY
3	B	MOVE UP ALL THE WAY
4	D	MOVE LEFT ALL THE WAY
5	C	MOVE RIGHT HALF THE WAY
6	C	MOVE LEFT HALF THE WAY
7	B	MOVE UP HALF THE WAY
8	B	MOVE DOWN HALF THE WAY
9	D	MOVE DOWN HALF THE WAY
10	C	MOVE UP ALL THE WAY
11	D	MOVE LEFT HALF THE WAY
12	B	MOVE DOWN ALL THE WAY ** Pay attention to color in "D" **
13	C	NOVE DOWN HALF THE WAY
14	C	MOVE RIGHT HALF THE WAY
15	A	MOVE RIGHT ALL THE WAY

SWAP

QUESTION #	ANSWER	ANALOGY
1	B	SEND BACK (SWAP POSITION)
2	A	SWAP COLOR
3	C	SWAP PLACE
4	B	SWAP COLOR
5	A	SWAP COLOR
6	D	SWAP COLOR ** Note: Analogy could be Flip sideways. But "B" is not Flipped
7	A	SWAP COLOR
8	D	SWAP COLOR
9	C	SEND BACK (SWAP POSITION)
10	A	SEND BACK (SWAP POSITION)
11	B	SEND BACK (SWAP POSITION)
12	B	SEND BACK (SWAP POSITION)
13	C	SEND BACK (SWAP POSITION)
14	A	SEND BACK (SWAP POSITION) Note: Colors of figures in example Analogy are NOT transparent
15	B	SWAP PLACE (and SIZE)
16	A	SWAP PLACE (and SIZE)
17	C	SWAP PLACE (and SIZE) Note: Analogy can be "Swap Color". But no right answer. B is not correct.
18	A	SWAP PLACE (and SIZE) and COLOR
19	B	SEND BACK (SWAP POSITION)
20	C	SWAP PLACE (and SIZE) and COLOR

TURN

QUESTION #	ANSWER	ANALOGY
1	C	TURN CLOCKWISE
2	A	TURN COUNTER CLOCKWISE
3	B	TURN CLOCKWISE
4	C	TURN COUNTER CLOCKWISE
5	D	TURN CLOCKWISE
6	B	TURN COUNTER CLOCKWISE
7	B	TURN CLOCKWISE
8	A	TURN CLOCKWISE
9	B	TURN CLOCKWISE Note: Example Analogy work for both clockwise and counter clockwise.
10	C	TURN COUNTER CLOCKWISE
11	A	TURN CLOCKWISE Note: Easy way to see turn is MOVE one base
12	B	TURN COUNTER CLOCKWISE Note: Easy way to see turn is MOVE one base
13	A	TURN CLOCKWISE Note: B is not correct. Color of connecting strip is White.
14	D	TURN COUNTER CLOCKWISE
15	A	TURN CLOCKWISE Note: Example analogy can be "FLIP sideways". Answer "B" is incorrect. One Figure is sent back.
16	C	TURN CLOCKWISE

		Note: Example analogy can be "FLIP UPSIDE DOWN". But there is no answer choice for FLIP.
17	C	TURN CLOCKWISE Note: Easy way to see turn is MOVE one base
18	A	TURN COUNTER CLOCKWISE
19	C	TURN CLOCKWISE
20	B	TURN COUNTER CLOCKWISE
21	A	TURN CLOCKWISE
22	D	TURN COUNTER CLOCKWISE
23	B	TURN CLOCKWISE Note: Example Analogy can be "FLIP Sideways", But there is no answer choice for FLIP.
24	B	TURN COUNTER CLOCKWISE
25	A	TURN COUNTER CLOCKWISE
26	C	TURN COUNTER CLOCKWISE
27	D	TURN CLOCKWISE
28	C	TURN CLOCKWISE
29	B	TURN COUNTER CLOCKWISE
30	C	TURN CLOCKWISE. Note: "A" is not correct. Lines inside circle are not Turned.

FULL LENGTH PRACTICE TEST#1

QUESTION #	ANSWER	ANALOGY
1	C	1. SWAP COLOR 2. Inside Figure: FLIP UPSIDE DOWN 3. Inside Figure: Make Small
2	B	1. TURN COUNTER CLOCKWISE 2. CHANGE COLOR
3	D	1. CHANGE COLOR TO WHITE 2. Add a small white Circle in the middle
4	A	1. ADD A SIDE 2. CHANGE PATTERN TO HORIZONTAL LINES
5	D	1. SWAP COLORS 2. MOVE DOWN HALF WAY
6	C	1. Outside Figure: Change Color Pattern to Vertical Lines 2. Add same figure as Outside with white color
7	B	1. Stretch Horizontally 2. Change Color Pattern to Vertical Lines
8	B	1. Outside Figure: Turn Counter Clockwise 2. Outside Figure: Change Color to WHITE 3. Add a shape inside
9	C	1. Outside Figure: Turn Clockwise 2. Inside Figure: Flip Upside Down 3. Inside Figure: Change Color to GRAY
10	A	1. Hexagon has 6 sides. ADD 6 small Hexagons of same color (GRAY)

11	D	1. Turn Clockwise 2. Change White-Color Figure Color to "Dotted Pattern"
12	D	1. Cut Diagonally Top 2. Change Pattern to Diagonal lines Note: Pattern is incorrect in answer choice "A"
13	C	1. Squeeze Horizontally 2. Add 2 figures of resulting shape
14	C	1. Bottom Figure: Remove 6 sides 2. Top Figure: Flip sideways 3. Note: Answer "B" is incorrect because its White COLOR.
15	D	1. Outside Figure: Add one more side 2. Inside Figure: Change Color to Dotted pattern.
16	B	1. Outside Figure: Turn Clockwise 2. Add same resulting figure inside with BLACK Color Note: Outside Figure can be FLIP sideways, but there is no correct answer choice
17	B	1. SWAP COLOR
18	B	1. Turn Clockwise 2. Make Small
19	C	1. Move Bottom Figure to Top (Change order of Figures)
20	A	1. White Figure: Flip Upside Down 2. Black Figure: Flip Sideway

FULL LENGTH PRACTICE TEST#2

QUESTION #	ANSWER	ANALOGY
1	D	SWAP COLORS
2	C	TURN CLOCKWISE
3	A	SEND BACK (SWAP POSITION)
4	A	CUT BOTTOM or MAKE SMALL
5	A	ADD A WHITE CIRCLE IN THE MIDDLE
6	B	FLIP UPSIDE DOWN
7	C	1. FLIP UPSIDE DOWN 2. MAKE ONE FIGURE BIG
8	D	SWAP COLORS
9	C	1. TURN CLOCKWISE 2. SWAP COLORS
10	B	ADD A SMALL FIGURE of Same Given Figure with Black Color and Flipped Upside down.
11	D	ADD VERTICAL LINES TO GIVEN FIGURE
12	B	ADD 3 MORE SIDES
13	B	ADD A WHITE SMALL FIGURE inside same as Outside Shape
14	A	FLIP. Note: FLIP SIDEWAYS is most SPECIFIC analogy. But there is no correct answer. Generic answer is FLIP.
15	D	FLIP UPSIDE DOWN
16	A	SWAP COLORS
17	C	MOVE HALF WAY TO LEFT

18	B	MOVE THE RIGHT MOST FIGURE TO LEFT MOST (CHANGE ORDER)
19	A	COMBINE 2 GIVEN FIGURES AND REMOVE INSIDE LINE
20	C	ADD SAME SHAPE PERPENDICULAR TO FIRST SHAPE

Other ways to use this book

Mini Practice Tests

Questions are organized by each individual concept. Picking 15 questions randomly and solving them out of order serve as a mini practice test. **About 12 mini practice tests** can be generated.

200 Additional Questions

After solving each question, Write down the answer in the box with **"?"**.

Now cover RIGHT box on EXAMPLE Analogy

This will form a different question.

Solve each question.

Additional Help

Have a question? You can reach author directly at
mindmineauthor@gmail.com

Made in the USA
Coppell, TX
09 September 2020

37453939R10105